TAMMY COHEN

TRUE STORIES OF LOVE, RECONCILIATION AND MURDER THAT STARTED WITH A CLICK

JOHN BLAKE

Published by John Blake Publishing Ltd,
3 Bramber Court, 2 Bramber Road,
London W14 9PB, England

www.johnblakepublishing.co.uk

First published in paperback in 2009

ISBN: 978 1 84454 638 1

British Library Cataloguing-in-Publication Data:

A catalogue record for this book is available from the British Library.

Design by www.envydesign.co.uk

Printed in Great Britain by CPI Bookmarque, Croydon CR0 4TD

1 3 5 7 9 10 8 6 4 2

Papers used by John Blake Publishing are natural, recyclable products
made from wood grown in sustainable forests. The manufacturing processes
conform to the environmental regulations of the country of origin.

Every attempt has been made to contact the relevant copyright-holders,
but some were unobtainable. We would be grateful if the appropriate
people could contact us.

FOR MICHAEL

PREFACE

The first time I ever heard of a website you could use to trace old classmates was when Helen, a friend I'd been in touch with periodically since school, got in touch in 2001.

'I've had the most traumatic few months,' she confided.

I was taken aback. Since starting up her own successful direct marketing company, Helen seemed to have led a charmed life, marrying Ed, one of her wealthy clients, and going on to have three small children in quick succession.

'It started when I looked up our old class on Friends Reunited,' she told me, surprised that she had to explain what it was.

'One of the people on the list was Tom R.' As she said his name, a vague memory stirred in my head of a dark-haired boy with scabby knees and so many freckles, his face looked permanently tanned.

'Well, we got "chatting" online, and before I knew it we were exchanging up to fifty emails a day. It was the most bizarre thing. We didn't really know each other at all, but it was as though because we'd known each other since we were six, we could talk to each other about anything. He was unhappily married and talked a lot about wanting to leave his wife, but being too scared of losing his children. It was so intimate so quickly. Before I really knew what was happening, we were talking about being in love.'

I couldn't believe it. Helen had always seemed so happy with Ed. It just didn't seem possible that she could have fallen for a guy she hadn't seen in over 25 years. Particularly, now I came to think of it, one whose mum had made him wear a white vest under his school shirt, summer and winter. But, apparently she had. Not only that, but they'd ended up spending a weekend together and made plans to leave their respective spouses and set up home together.

Except that Tom R's wife had found out where he was and who he was with, and rang Ed, who left a message on Helen's phone.

'He told me not to bother coming back.' Even over the phone, I could sense the shudder in Helen's voice as she remembered receiving the message. 'All of a sudden it became real. It was like I'd been woken up from a trance and I felt sick at the thought that I'd been ready to trade in my family for a guy I hardly knew. Tom clearly felt the same. He and I could hardly bear to look at each other. He had packed up his stuff within minutes of getting off the phone to his wife, and was sitting on the edge of the bed with his head in his hands.'

Before they parted, Tom and Helen gave each other an awkward kiss and promised to keep in touch, but both knew they wouldn't be seeing each other again. Helen went home and begged Ed for another chance, but even when I spoke to her seven months later, things hadn't quite returned to normal.

'He says he's forgiven me, but he'll never forget. I don't suppose we'll ever get back the trust we had before,' Helen told me sadly. 'Now, when I look back on what happened, I just can't believe it. It was like, for a few mad weeks, I became someone else.'

Which is, in essence, exactly what happened. Helen became someone else – the child she used to be, with a child's passionate, selfish impulses and disregard for consequences. Whether it was a subconscious reaction to getting married, with all its attendant adult responsibilities, or just a response to the seductive *Wuthering Heights* notion that only someone who knew you in childhood can truly be a soul mate, Helen had attempted to step back into the past and had only just managed to return in the nick of time.

I knew then that this notion of reuniting old friends was powerful stuff. For many it's a welcome bridge between past and present, a way of bringing new experience and maturity to bear on old friends and old memories. But it wasn't until I was doing research for my true-crime anthologies, and came across a number of cases involving social networking websites, that I realised just how dangerous meddling with the past could be.

Since that initial phone conversation with Helen, there has been an explosion of social networking sites that aim not only to reunite us with our severed past, but also to ensure the past becomes obsolete entirely. Like it or not, we need never lose touch with anyone again. Even if we expunge them from our friends' list, some mutual connection will ensure they can always keep tabs on us, monitoring what we get up to, remaining part of our lives for as long as they wish to be. That is the beauty – and the danger – of networking.

Writing this book, I've come across people who've been reunited with family members or reintroduced to the love of their lives. There are people who've got married because of these networking sites, and babies who owe their very existence to them. There are even two childhood friends who, thanks to a networking site, were reunited in time to undergo life-saving transplant surgery.

On the flip side, I've also heard from families torn apart, marriages ripped to shreds and normally sane human beings brought to within an inch of madness.

*   *   *

Some of the dialogue represented in this book was sourced from available documents, some was drawn from tape-recorded testimony and some was reconstructed from the memory of participants. That means making informed deductions for dramatic purposes. Occasionally, names have been changed for legal reasons. But the actual facts are as they occurred.

The past is a Pandora's box. Anyone who opens it up should be prepared for a few surprises.

Tammy Cohen 2009

CONTENTS

INTRODUCTION

The past is a foreign country. Or at least, it used to be. Nowadays, however, with the advent of social networking websites such as Friends Reunited, Facebook and MySpace, it's a country for which we all have dual nationality.

Never has it been so easy to access the selves we thought we left behind in playgrounds, classrooms and Friday-night bus shelters. Never have so many childhood friends, long forgotten, been brought so vividly back to life, trailing divorces, children, sagging paunches and receding hairlines in their wakes.

Quite simply, with the help of the World Wide Web, we've found a way if not of halting time's winged chariot, then at least making it double back for a while. By getting in touch with the ghosts of our childhood selves, we get a second chance at being young, a second chance to exorcise the classroom demons and put right bitterly stored-up wrongs. With the click of a mouse, we once again rediscover the door in the wall, long grown-over, which leads back into the rose garden.

No wonder when the original social networking site, Friends Reunited, was set up in 2000 we signed up in our droves. Within two years of starting up from Steve and Julie Pankhurst's back room in Barnet, north London, more than seven million people had registered, with 15,000 more joining every day.

Find out what your old classmates are up to now, get in touch with childhood friends, rekindle playground romances... for a generation who'd grown up with the maxim that life gives no second chances, it was too seductive a promise to resist.

All over the country, reunions were organised, old friends re-contacted, email relationships established. Who wouldn't want to know whether the class bully got her comeuppance, or whether the school sweethearts ended up tying the knot? Who wouldn't relish the chance of putting their best selves forward to show how far they'd come? Who could resist the opportunity of measuring themselves against their peers to see how they matched up?

For a while, Friends Reunited was a brand-new toy that the whole country was playing with. Friendships, long discarded, were picked up and dusted off, and declared to be a perfect fit, even after all these years. More importantly, innocent childhood crushes were brought back to life, with the added element of maturity and adult sexuality. It wasn't long before the site was boasting its first wedding and its first baby.

The beauty of it lay in its informality. You didn't have to come up with a convoluted explanation for wanting to revisit the past, nor did you have to go into too much detail about your own life, or anyone else's. Everything was done for you, so you could give away as little or as much as you liked. There was no emotional investment, no whiff of desperation. The past could be laid bare with the same casual flick of a computer mouse, as if you were ordering your groceries online.

By the time Friends Reunited celebrated its seventh birthday in 2007, it boasted 12 million members and had gone from a family-run labour of love to a multimillion-pound-making business venture that had been bought up by ITV.

Naturally, success spawned imitators and rivals. Other social networking sites sprang up – MySpace, Facebook, Bebo – less fixated upon the past, but still offering the same chance to stay in touch with old friends you might otherwise have outgrown.

And of course, it wasn't long before the shiny new surface of the nation's favourite new toy began to tarnish. Relationship counsellors began to report a worrying new trend towards online infidelity between recently reconnected childhood sweethearts. It seemed the combination of nostalgia, plus an urge to go back to a more uncomplicated time, was powerfully seductive. Throw into that mix the thrill of being with a person who remembers you when you had promise and ambition, not to mention all your own hair, and you have a recipe for instant attraction.

Hot on the heels of the first Friends Reunited weddings, came the first Friends Reunited divorces. And it didn't stop there.

Inevitably, where there's sex and betrayal, there will eventually come hatred and revenge. The first website-inspired murders began to hit the headlines. Betrayed spouses, unable to bear the pain of being ditched by long-term partners in favour of hastily rekindled childhood romances, took the law into their own hands. In 2006, wealthy businesswoman Ann Hunter was jailed for trying to recruit a hitman to murder her ex-husband's new wife, a former college sweetheart he'd contacted through Friends Reunited. The same year, farmer Martin Baker was found guilty of murdering his wife Tina, who had left him for a man she'd met at a Friends Reunited-inspired school reunion. As her body was never found, it was speculated that Baker had fed her to his pigs.

In May 2008, Tracey Grinhaff, a mother-of-two from Wombwell in Yorkshire, was found dead after using her

Facebook page to inform old friends that she was splitting up with her husband, Gary. It was believed that grief-stricken Gary killed his wife before going on to take his own life.

Wayne Forrester was similarly driven to murder after his estranged wife changed her Facebook status to 'single'.

In the natural order of things, we move through life shedding some friendships naturally like sloughing off dead skin, as we change and grow, but social networking sites have changed all that. How is it possible to put the past behind you when, at any moment, the past can find out whom you've been seeing and what you had for dinner, or poring over photos of your shiny new life?

Not only do these websites keep you in touch with people you might actually prefer to leave behind, they also provide the perfect tool for revenge – allowing disgruntled exes instant access to your friends' network, and therefore maximum potential for public humiliation. Two of the cases featured here were men found guilty after setting up false and sexually explicit accounts in their ex-girlfriends' names on different social networking websites.

But it isn't only affairs of the heart that have got the social networking sites into the newspapers. There have been cases of old childhood feuds being resumed, teachers suing for defamation of character, people being unmasked as fantasists, bigamists and fraudsters.

On the positive side, there have also been heart-warming stories of divided families finding one another again, of lonely elderly widows finding unexpected comfort in long-lost girlhood friends.

You used to be able to draw a line under the past, but with the help of the World Wide Web, and social networking sites, that line has become either blurred or else completely erased. You can never completely outgrow your childhood if it's likely to send you a message direct to your inbox or invite you to a 25th-anniversary school reunion.

The truth is that social networking sites provide us with the chance to rewrite our own histories. Where once we were shy, awkward, underachieving, now we can prove ourselves successful, witty and popular. We can surround ourselves with ghosts of a time when life was simpler and ourselves less careworn. We can reignite fires of passion we never realised had been smouldering within us for years, even decades. We can find lovers, friends, sisters, mothers, with just one tap of a key, one press of a mouse.

And if we also take the opportunity to settle old scores, or inadvertently break up new marriages, well that's the pay-off, isn't it, for daring to re-create what has passed?

The past is no longer a foreign country. The borders are down; anybody is free to cross over. For good or for bad, our lives will never be quite the same again.

xx

CHAPTER ONE

'AFTER 25 YEARS OF LOOKING, I FOUND MY KIDS ONLINE'

Pulling up in the car outside the unfamiliar house in the subdued half-light of a dull November day, Ray Rose – a man not normally given to extreme displays of emotion – was astonished to find himself trembling uncontrollably. For 25 years he'd dreamed of this moment, running different scenarios through his head like flowing water, soothing his doubts and fears by telling himself over and over that it would happen eventually. He couldn't believe, after all this time, that the moment had finally arrived.

For a few seconds after the car engine was turned off, there was a silence in which nothing stirred and time seemed frozen. Glancing over towards the house, Ray could see the door had opened and there were two figures standing there – a man in the front, tall with

1

brown hair, and behind him, craning to see, a woman wearing an anxious smile. It couldn't be… could it?

'You get out first, love,' he told his wife Cherry, who had already opened her door and was looking over towards the house, a broad grin spreading over her face.

As Cherry made her way up the path, Ray followed behind on legs that were shaking with nerves. In his pocket he could feel the wallet that contained the dog-eared photos he'd carried with him for the last two-and-a-half decades. A little boy with a cheeky grin and a mop of blond hair, and a girl, still just a toddler, with plump baby cheeks. It didn't seem possible that the grown man and woman he saw ahead of him could have anything to those faded images, worn with time and over-handling. And yet almost immediately he could see a resemblance. Looking at the tall man in the front was like looking at a mirror into the past where his own 33-year-old self looked back at him.

Finally, after what seemed like hours, but could only have been a few seconds, he and Cherry were at the door, his legs now feeling as if they were going to give way under him.

'Hello,' he croaked nervously, looking from the man to the woman and then back again, his own voice sounding strange in his ears.

'I'm Ray. I'm your dad.'

* * *

Ray Rose had never meant to be an absentee father. The birth of his son, Graham, in 1974 had been the proudest moment of his life. As he'd looked down at the tiny creature in his arms, a little hand clutching hard around his finger, he'd imagined a future bursting with football in the park on Sunday mornings and tea-times doing homework around the kitchen table. He'd envisaged putting plasters on grazed knees and cheering from the sidelines at school soccer matches. Further ahead, he could picture himself sitting in the car outside school discos – hidden from view, of course (you know how teenagers get) – waiting to drive his son home and meeting his first girlfriend, wondering whether she was good enough for him.

Isn't it funny how real life can muck up all our best-laid plans?

Ray had met Graham's mother, Barbara, while they were both very young and living on the same street in Carshalton in Surrey. As newlyweds, they'd moved to Milton Keynes, which, in those days, was a brand-new town and one of the few places a young couple like them could afford to get a house. New house, new family – the future then had seemed fresh and dewy with promise.

Yet within a few months of Graham's birth, the sheen had started to come off their bright new future. Barbara had suffered from post-natal depression after Graham's birth, finding even the smallest of everyday tasks a burden, and the young family ended up moving back to Carshalton to live with Barbara's mother and brother so that she had some family support.

For Ray, it was a very stressful time. While he knew his wife needed to be looked after, he couldn't help feeling pushed out as Barbara's mother and brother took over the day-to-day responsibility of looking after Graham. He too found himself growing increasingly depressed as he saw his role as a father being gradually eroded away. Unable to cope with the strain, Ray eventually moved out to his mother's house nearby, although he and Barbara continued to see each other.

By the time Karen was born, in 1976, it was clear there were very deep problems in the marriage. The couple were living apart and Ray increasingly felt superfluous to requirements as far as his children were concerned. Barbara's family made it clear they had everything under control and he felt useless and unneeded – more like visitor than a parent.

Inevitably, he and Barbara drifted apart and when she met someone else a couple of years after Karen was born, they divorced. Ray still had access to his children, but each time he visited, he felt less welcome than the last. Often when he called round, there'd be an excuse about why he couldn't see the children: one of them was ill; they were napping. Every now and then, he'd manage to get to take the kids out – Graham loved being taken down to Gatwick to watch the planes – but there was never any regularity in the arrangement. The visits grew increasingly sporadic and, when they happened at all, Ray felt more and more like an outsider.

Barbara was still seeing her new man and, to Ray's distress, the two of them decided to move back to Milton Keynes, taking the children with them. Ray still had legal visiting rights, but when Barbara changed her surname without telling him and then moved house without giving him a forwarding address, he realised he had no way of enforcing the court ruling, or indeed of finding out where they'd gone. He travelled up to Milton Keynes, looking around places he and Barbara had visited together, but there was no trace. His children had disappeared.

Ever more depressed and stressed, Ray couldn't work. At home, lonely and desperate, he'd gaze for hours at the photos of his children, wondering what they were doing at that moment, trying to imagine how they might have changed.

When he looked back on the pride he'd felt at Graham's birth, and the dreams he'd had of their future, it felt like he was remembering someone else, some stranger. Now each morning it was a struggle to get out of bed and each day went passed with agonising slowness, the empty hours stretching endlessly onwards.

Eventually, though, Ray started to rebuild his

shattered life, piece by piece. He moved to Suffolk and got a job working for a courier company driving parcels and packages round Suffolk and the south-east. He also met Cherry, a divorcee with two children, whom he married in 1992. But while he learned to enjoy life again, there was always something missing. Watching Cherry's children – a boy and a girl more or less the same ages as Graham and Karen – growing older only reminded Ray of all he was missing out on in his own children's lives.

The milestones – Christmas, Father's Day, each of his children's birthdays – were the worst. Those were the days he'd wake up wondering what they were up to, these phantom children who'd remained for him forever frozen in time at the ages he'd last seen them, all baby hair and dimples. Although he told himself not to be so stupid, he couldn't help wondering on these kind of anniversaries whether this year would be the year his kids got in touch, whether this year he'd open the post to find a Christmas card written in a childish hand, or a shyly worded Father's Day card. But it never happened.

One day, he bumped into Barbara's brother. Although they'd never been close, they had a chat and he discovered Barbara had moved with the kids down to Eastbourne, though her brother and mother had lost touch with her soon afterwards.

For a while Ray was excited, as his job regularly took

him to that area. He began stopping off every time he had a delivery to the south-east coast and trawling the streets looking for any clue as to where his family had gone. But it was hopeless. All he had were the photos, now creased with time, of his children as babies. Of course, they'd be unrecognisable now. The few people he approached on the off chance just shrugged pityingly and walked on.

And so the years passed and Ray got so used to living with loss that the hole at the centre of his life barely registered with him any more. That's not to say he didn't think about his kids – he thought about them every day – more that their absence became integral to who he was.

Every now and then something would happen that would send hope suddenly flaring up inside him, searing in its intensity. When computers became commonplace, bringing with them access to a world of information, Ray felt a surge of optimism. Surely this was a way of getting in touch with Graham and Karen again?

Several times, he went to the local library to make use of the computers there. By this time he'd left his job after damaging his spine so he had plenty of free time, but each time he came away despondent. With each session lasting just half an hour and no formal computer training, it seemed he'd hardly managed to turn the machine on before it was time to log off again. The Internet, with its complicated search engines and endless lists of results, defeated him, and he'd slink away from the row of terminals in the library with a heavy heart, laden with longing.

In 2004, increasingly desperate, Ray contacted *The Trisha Show*, hoping against hope that the programme's team of researchers might be able to dig up some information on his missing kids. For weeks after he'd told them every bit of information he had, he waited by the phone, hoping for news. But when the call came, it was yet another disappointment. They hadn't been able to find any leads.

Then, at the beginning of October 2007, Ray received a present. Cherry, knowing how much he yearned to find out what had become of his children, had bought him a laptop computer to help him with his search. Freed from time pressures, Ray was able to start negotiating his way painstakingly around the Net, gradually discovering which sites might be best to start looking for his kids.

At first, he aimed at sites that catered solely for finding missing family members, but every time his hopes were raised, they were quickly dashed again when search after search drew a blank. The problem was that, without a surname, there was just no way to trace the two smiling childish ghosts of his memory.

Then, on 5 November, Guy Fawkes night, Ray was messing around on the computer as usual and decided to log onto Friends Reunited. He'd already joined up looking for old school friends and wanted to check if anyone else was listed. After browsing his school page, he idly started looking through the rest of the site and noticed there was a facility that could put you in touch with people who'd lived on your street.

That captured his imagination. Immediately he was transported back to the Carshalton street where he'd grown up. He could hear the sounds of the kids playing outside on their bikes, the voices of neighbours calling to each other over back fences. He remembered traipsing up and down every inch of that road on his way to and from school, bag laden with books, heart light with optimism. Nostalgia pressed in around him as he slowly keyed the name of the road into his laptop.

After a few seconds' wait, a list of names appeared of other people who'd registered as having lived on that road over the years. One name in particular stood out. Susan. Barbara's sister.

For a long time, Ray just stared at the name, surprised by the force of emotion it stirred up. It was like this whenever he saw anything that reminded him of his children. The immediate raw jolt of pain that seemed to come from nowhere.

Susan, it appeared, was now living in Scotland. Ray didn't really hold out much hope for a response, but she was a connection to his kids, someone who might know where they were, or at least where they'd been lately. It was worth a shot.

With hesitant fingers, still unfamiliar with the layout of the keyboard, Ray painstakingly typed out his request. He was desperate, he told his former sister-in-law. He'd searched all these years for some clue as to where his children might be. Did she have any idea? Any suggestion where he could start looking? He'd never given up wanting to see them.

He told himself not to get his hopes up. He'd been disappointed so many times in the past. She probably wouldn't even reply.

When, a short time later, Susan's name popped up in his inbox, he could hardly believe it. His heart started hammering inside his chest as he opened up the message and read slowly through.

Are you the same Ray who married my sister? Susan wanted to know. If so, she went on, she was prepared to get in touch with Graham and, provided he was willing, would forward his number to Ray.

Shaking, Ray read through the message again and again, certain he must have misunderstood, not daring to believe it might actually be as easy as that. Surely, after two-and-a-half decades of waiting, his long search couldn't be about to be settled with just one tiny click of a computer mouse?

He called Cherry over and she read through the

message with him, realising immediately just what it meant. 'Go on then,' she urged him. 'Send her a message. What are you waiting for?'

Obediently, Ray wrote back, asking her to contact Graham on his behalf, each word seeming to take forever with his slow, laborious typing. Then, with a deep breath, he hit 'send'.

There followed the most agonising wait. It was as if everything over the last 25 years had been leading up to this moment and now, just as things were moving forward, suddenly time was suspended. The very air around them seemed weighted down, swollen with expectation.

When a second message from Susan popped up into the inbox, Ray could hardly bring himself to open it. When he finally did, he again had to read and re-read it several times before finally taking in what it was saying.

'Here's Graham's number,' Susan had written. 'He's waiting for you to call.'

But now that the moment was finally here, now that the opportunity he'd been wishing for all these years had finally fallen into his lap, he found himself suddenly unable to act. 'I don't think I can do it,' he whispered hoarsely to Cherry. 'You ring him.'

But Cherry was equally nervous. 'It's not me he wants to talk to,' she told him.

Realising Ray was shaking too much to make the call, Cherry finally picked up the phone and, with hesitant fingers, dialled the number Susan had written in her message. It could only have been ringing for a second or two, although to Ray it felt like an eternity, before Cherry started speaking.

'Hello? Is that Graham? Graham, I've got your dad here.'

Your dad. How long had he waited to hear that phrase? Ray's hand was trembling as he picked up the receiver.

'I've searched for you for over 25 years,' he managed to croak.

An unfamiliar male voice, equally knotted with emotion replied: 'And we've been looking for you.'

It was finally here – the moment Ray had been dreaming of for all those years. He was actually talking to his son. It seemed so surreal. The last time he'd spoken to Graham he was eight years old; now there was this 33-year-old man's voice on the end of the phone. 'I can't believe I'm talking to you,' he stuttered, shell-shocked. 'After all this time.'

Graham told him how he and Karen, who hadn't had the happiest of childhoods, had tried to find him, even though their mother had tried to persuade them not to. 'Don't bother trying to find him,' she'd warned them. 'He won't want to know you.' But they'd come up against the same brick walls as he had. They hadn't even known his surname until Graham had registered to get married and had been asked which name he wanted to use. 'What do you mean, which name?' he'd asked, flummoxed, only to be told he had another surname in addition to that of his stepfather. Rose. For the first time, he'd known his father's name. 'I decided then and there to change my surname back to Rose,' Graham told an increasingly choked-up Ray.

In all, Ray was on the phone to his son for an hour that night, talking – once the initial awkwardness was over – about everything under the sun. By the time he put the phone down, he was so dazed, he could hardly think. It just didn't seem possible that this was happening to him. But he'd hardly begun to tell Cherry about his conversation with Graham when the phone went again. This time it was a woman's voice on the phone: Karen. 'Graham just rang me,' she said, unable to hide the excitement in her voice. 'I can't believe it.'

Ray was already fighting back the tears at speaking to his daughter again, who'd been hardly more than a baby when he last saw her. Then she said something that pushed him right over the edge.

'Do you know you've got six grandchildren?'

Now Ray really was lost for words. His mouth was dry and he felt his legs about to give way. *Six grandchildren.* Plus, so Karen went on to tell him, another one on the way. Just a couple of hours ago, he'd had no blood family and now he had children and grandchildren. It seemed so incredible, like something from a television show. Only when he gazed across at Cherry, through eyes blurry with tears, and found her beaming at him in delight, did it begin to sink in. This was actually happening. He'd found them at last.

For an hour and a half, Ray chatted to the woman he'd last seen as a toddler. Both of them were by turns tearful, then laughing as they tried to piece together the missing years that had defined both their lives. When he eventually put the phone down, he felt as if every conceivable emotion had been squeezed out of him drop by drop, leaving him drained and dazed but nevertheless elated. 'I can't believe it,' he kept repeating to Cherry as the bangs from distant fireworks sounded outside the window. 'I just can't believe it.'

Just two days after that momentous night, Ray and Cherry were in the car on their way down to Eastbourne. Watching the landscape go past in a blur of grass embankments and motorway service stations, Ray couldn't help thinking back to those other times when he'd driven down this same route, his precious photos safely stashed in his wallet, hoping against hope that this would be the day he found out something, anything, about his children. And he thought about all those journeys back, his heart leaden, hopes yet again dashed.

How different it was now, driving down with Cherry by his side holding on her lap the carefully copied directions to Karen's house. Soon he'd be meeting his son and daughter. But even though he kept reminding himself of that, the niggling doubts refused to completely disappear. After so many years of false hopes and dead-end trails, it seemed inconceivable that he was about to get the one thing that had eluded him all this time.

As the car made its way down unfamiliar Eastbourne streets, Ray started to realise it wasn't going to be quite as straightforward as he'd hoped. In fact, he was lost. They retraced their route and tried to find where they'd gone wrong, all the time conscious of the ticking clock and all the precious time that was being wasted.

They'd just found the right road when Ray's mobile started ringing.

'Where are you?' came Graham's anxious voice. When Ray told him they'd got lost but had sorted themselves out, his son didn't try to hide his relief. 'Thank goodness for that. We thought you'd been having second thoughts.' Second thoughts! As if the greatest powers on earth could have kept Ray away from keeping this particular appointment.

Finally, they were pulling up outside a terraced house where, immediately, the door was flung open wide. And there were Graham and Karen standing anxiously on the step, craning to get a proper look at the man whose trembling legs would hardly carry him up the path.

How do you condense two-and-a-half decades of

hopes and dreams into a single moment? What words do you say to make up for a lifetime of enforced silence?

Standing awkwardly by the door, Ray shyly introduced himself and Cherry to these two strangers who, nevertheless, seemed somehow instantly familiar. And they were in turn introduced to Graham and Karen's partners. And then there was a commotion as all the grandchildren, who'd been standing impatiently behind their parents, decided they'd had enough of waiting and came out to inspect their new granddad.

The children's excitement soon overrode any nerves the adults might have had and before long they were all talking ten to the dozen, as if sheer volume of words could somehow make up for all the lost time.

Karen and Graham spoke about their childhoods and how they'd been told their father didn't want anything to do with them. In turn, Ray told them how he'd fought to stay in contact with them, and how hard he'd tried to find them. 'I wish this could have happened years ago,' Graham said sadly, as Ray's visit came to an end.

Ray nodded, and for a moment he was bitter all over again about the years that had been denied to them. 'But we can't afford to think like that,' he said quickly. 'We've got to start looking forward to the future, instead of feeling sad about the past.'

Long before he and Cherry left to drive back to Suffolk, they'd all arranged to meet up again, not willing to risk another separation without being sure of a definite end to it.

As soon as he got home, Ray sent both his children a text. Not a man given to flamboyant shows of emotion, he nevertheless needed to convey to them just how much this meeting had meant to him. 'I'm so proud to have you as my children,' he told them both.

After that, the three were rarely out of contact. If lost time could be restored by effort and will alone, they would surely have clawed back their missing years. Karen texted Ray every day, including him in the trivia of her day so that he felt he was a part of her life. Graham would call him to complain he had a cold coming, or his back was hurting – little things that a son would tell a parent when he was growing up, things that he'd missed telling his dad when he was a child.

And there were many more meetings. After that first uncertain journey, Ray came to know the route to his kids' homes in Eastbourne very well. It never failed to give him a thrill to pull up outside a house and know that in seconds he'd be seeing his children. But there was still an occasional ache of regret that he knew would never quite disappear. Sometimes when he watched Graham playing with one of his own children, he'd feel a stab of anguish that he himself had been denied the chance to play with his kids like that, their squeals of laughter triggering some deep well of happiness inside himself. At other times he'd find himself gazing at Graham and Karen, trying to recognise their younger selves in these startlingly adult people.

Christmas 2007 was a very different affair to the years that had preceded it. For once Ray didn't experience the daily dampening of hope every time the post came and went without a card from his missing kids. For once he didn't wake up on Christmas morning, wondering where they were and what they were doing. Instead, he and Cherry went down to Eastbourne just before Christmas, laden with presents for the grandchildren.

He knew Graham and Karen, with young families to support, didn't have much money, so he wasn't expecting a gift. Which is why he was surprised when, with barely suppressed excitement, they slipped a package into his hands.

'You shouldn't have...' he began. But his protests were cut short.

'Open it!' came a chorus of impatient voices.

Carefully sliding open the wrapping, at first Ray couldn't understand what the commotion was about. It was a perfectly ordinary-looking calendar for the following year, 2008. But as he opened it, he suddenly choked up inside.

Every page featured a different photo of his children and grandchildren, together with a caption detailing when it was taken. Some were recent pictures, others went way back to when Graham and Karen were growing up. After all those years of carrying round those old dog-eared snapshots with their baby faces, it was like having a little bit of their childhood restored to him.

Looking around at the faces lit up with expectation, Ray could hardly speak for the unexpected emotion that threatened to overwhelm him. He hadn't just found his family, he'd also found a thread connecting him to the past and providing him with a stake in the future.

*   *   *

Over the past months, Ray's relationship with his newfound family seems to strengthen every day. He may have missed out on many of the big events in their lives, but in sharing the day-to-day trivia of his children's days, they're weaving a new family tapestry, richer in texture and colour than any of them could have dreamed possible.

And while it's tempting to look back bitterly on all the lost years, Ray is determined to focus on the planning for the future rather than pining for the past.

'We've got so much time to make up,' he says, the legacy of his two-and-a-half-decade search still clearly etched in his face. 'I spent 25 years looking for my children. Who'd have thought, after all the miles I covered, I'd have found them through a website? But now we're back together again, I'm determined to be there for them for the rest of my life.'

CHAPTER TWO
'I AM AN EXECUTIONER'

Susan Matta took a deep breath, taking in the smell of fresh paint and new carpet. Sometimes it still seemed as though this must all be a dream – the boxes still piled up in the hallway, the 'Sold' signs just visible through the window in the front gardens of the other houses on the new development. And, most unbelievable of all, there was Stephen.

Every time she looked at Stephen, Susan was struck all over again by that jolt of surprise. He was practically a stranger, this middle-aged man with his glasses and his receding hairline. And yet at the same time he was so achingly, comfortably familiar. Just being with him felt like being home, even in the alien surroundings of this brand-new house they'd just bought together.

And when he smiled at her, as he so often did, he was

no longer a 54-year-old man with greying hair, but the teenager he'd been when they first met all those years before. And the Susan she saw reflected back at her in his eyes wasn't a careworn 53-year-old woman with two failed marriages behind her, but the pretty, dark-haired schoolgirl from Devon who had her whole life ahead of her.

Once again she found herself sending up a silent prayer of thanks for the second chance she'd so unexpectedly been offered. So few people experience true love even once, but to let it go, and then have it so unexpectedly and magically restored to her still felt like a miracle. When she'd logged onto that website just a few months before and seen his name, it had felt as though the last thirty years had never happened. And in many ways, it felt like that still.

Of course, her happiness was tinged with guilt. More than anything she wished other people hadn't been hurt when she and Steve had fallen in love. Steve's wife, Doreen, her own husband, Francesco – neither had seen the bombshell coming and both were left struggling to come to terms with what had happened. If only they'd never let each other go the first time, how much heartache could have been saved?

But there was no point dwelling on 'if onlys'. Life wasn't a dress rehearsal and, as they all knew only too well, neither was it always fair. Against all the odds, she and Steve had found each other again and for the first time in decades, each felt complete. They were two halves of the same whole and they'd known almost immediately that they wanted to spend the rest of their lives together.

'I still can't believe we're both here,' she said again, for the hundredth time since moving into their new home eight days before.

Steve smiled. That same warm, wide smile which had caused her insides to melt when she first set eyes on him as a shy 14-year-old when they were both pupils at Tiverton Grammar School all those years before. Once again she found herself thinking that surely something that felt this right couldn't be wrong. Everything would work itself out. They just had to give everyone else time to readjust.

It was 6 July 2006. Devon, so sleepy during the winter months, was starting to stir itself into action in preparation for the summer season. All around was a palpable air of anticipation and promise, of tantalising new beginnings. Even their new house – one of several houses in a brand-new development – reflected the sense of being part of a shiny new future. When life offered you the chance of happiness, thought Susan, you owed it to yourself to grab it with both hands.

And yet, something was moving towards Susan that would drive a bulldozer over her new-found happiness.

Something was approaching through the warm July evening that would smash her shiny new future into a thousand pieces, until they lay scattered about her like fragments of a broken mirror.

For the last few days, her estranged Sardinian husband had been driving his rented van steadily across Europe – through Switzerland, France – edging onwards towards the UK, then on the slow, crowded roads towards Devon. Creeping, creeping, ever closer. On the seat next to him he had the usual detritus of a long journey – half-empty water bottle, the remains of a ferry ticket. Rather less predictable were the other objects he had brought with him, hidden from view. Pick-axe handle. Rope. Knife.

He was Franco Matta: hard-working postman, former chef, devoted husband.

He was also Franco Matta: the man in black, the executioner.

* * *

In the beginning, everything about having an Italian boyfriend had seemed thrillingly exotic. Francisco, or Franco as everyone called him, had been a chef for many years, so he cooked fantastic Italian food, and when he talked about the island of Sardinia, where he was from, it sounded like the most magical place on earth.

When Susan had first met him in 1999, two years after divorcing her first husband, with whom she had two grown-up children, she hadn't been looking for a serious relationship. Certainly not with a man who was himself only a year out of a long marriage.

But he'd been so kind and so full of life, with an infectious, raucous sense of humour and he had adored her from the outset, making her feel that perhaps it wasn't the end of the world to be 45 and single again and that she was still a desirable woman.

Franco had been living in Devon since 1971, when barely out of his teens, he'd decided to build a new life for himself in a country that offered more in the way of work opportunities than his own homeland. He'd started as a chef and it wasn't long before he'd acquired an Italian restaurant – Franco's, in Braunton, north Devon – and a local wife.

When his marriage broke up in 1998, leaving him middle-aged, miserable and unexpectedly single, there were times when he, like Susan, had wondered whether he'd ever find anyone else to love. So meeting Susan just a year later had been both a joy and a relief.

The couple quickly realised this was a relationship that brought them both enormous pleasure and they began to make plans for a future together. For the newly in love, there are few more enjoyable activities than idly plotting out different 'what if' scenarios – various enticing futures that they spread out in front of them to pick from like a box of chocolates.

What if we move to the country and open a B&B...? What if we buy a boat...? What if we throw it all in and travel the world...?

By the time they married in 2003, there was one 'what if' scenario Franco and Susan kept coming back to again and again. What if we move to Sardinia and get involved in letting out villas to tourists?

The more they talked about it, the more attractive the idea seemed. Susan's sons were grown-up and didn't need her as much, and after years of being a dutiful parent, she felt entitled to a little adventure. She imagined a slower, lazier pace of life, watching sunsets over velvet-blue Mediterranean waters, eating long lunches on sun-dappled restaurant terraces – salads made with fat olives and juicy tomatoes bought that morning from the local market.

And for a while after the newlywed couple moved to Cagliari in 2004, it really did seem as though life in the Sardianian capital was going to be every bit as idyllic as she'd imagined. Sardinia, the second largest Mediterranean island, is a favourite among well-heeled tourists who fall under the spell of its white-sand beaches and saltwater lagoons, its crystal waters and pine-clad hills. It boasts the sophisticated glamour of Italy mixed with the exoticism of Africa, to which it is marginally closer than Europe.

Cagliari, its principal city, is built on seven gentle hills that maximise the views of its stunning harbour and wide sandy bay. To Susan, her mind still full of the congested backroads and overcast skies of Devon, it was a different world with its elegant 19th-century streets shaded by jacaranda trees, and the upmarket palm-lined Via Roma with its chic designer shops.

At weekends, she and Franco, like many of the city's 200,000 or so residents, would sometimes take to the Poetto Beach to eat fresh fish at one of the beachside restaurants or just relax on the soft white sand. On fine evenings, they might have an ice-cream in one of the city's famous ice-cream parlours or stroll through the romantic piazzas.

But, as anyone who's ever lived abroad will tell you, there comes a point when the things that so enthral you while on holiday cease to hold the same attraction. Faced with endless sunshine, you start to miss the subtle seasonal changes of home. Anticipating the prospect of another pasta dish, or seafood platter, you long for an Indian curry or a Sunday roast lunch with all the trimmings.

Susan found herself becoming increasingly homesick. She'd started learning Italian back in the UK, but the strong Sardinian dialect proved impossible to master. With Franco working long hours in the postal service, she began to feel more and more isolated, and missed the friends and family she'd left behind in England.

At least there was the holiday lettings business to keep

her occupied. The only trouble was trying to make sure the villa they had to rent was consistently occupied outside of the main holiday season.

Susan knew the best way of generating interest was through word of mouth and personal recommendation, so she started to network online, sending emails to all her friends and acquaintances back in the UK describing the villa. Then one day, a short while after moving to Sardinia, she came up with an idea. Why not spread her network wider by joining up with Friends Reunited? That way, she got to kill two birds with one stone – she could satisfy her own curiosity about what her old classmates were up to and spread the word about the villa to a new potential market.

As soon as she logged onto her old school page on the site, she was immediately engulfed by a wave of nostalgia, made even more intense by her sense of isolation at being in this foreign country so far from home. All those familiar names, each one bringing to mind a different memory, a dusty image, faded by time but still recognisable. The girl she was. The life she'd had.

Trying not to get bogged down by nostalgia, she set her mind to business and posted an advert for the villa on the website, hoping it would generate some interest among people with whom she already shared common ground. Sure enough, enquiries came trickling in from people who either recognised her name, or were interested in finding out more about the villa. She started checking in regularly, just to see whether that day had brought any new messages cropping up in her mail box.

And then she saw it. Stephen Keen. The name that, more than any other, jolted her out of her current reality and sent her freefalling into the past. He'd been her first proper boyfriend, when she was just 14 and he a couple of years older. They'd been so close, sharing dreams for the future, taking long walks together and spending long summer days on the beach. But just before Steve joined the RAF while Susan was still at school, they'd had a minor tiff and the relationship had floundered.

Over the years, he'd crossed her mind more times than she cared to remember. But she'd squashed him back into the box marked 'the past'. He'd be married by now, she was sure of it. He'd probably have forgotten all about her.

Clearly he hadn't.

For a long time, Susan just stared at the name in her inbox, taken aback by the strength of her own reaction, lost in a fog of memories that came, unbidden into her mind – so many and so quickly that for a moment she lost sight of where she was.

Then she opened the email. It was chatty and friendly. Stephen asked if she could be the same Susan he'd gone to school with. He told her a little bit about what he'd been up to. It was lovely to hear from him, like putting a missing piece in a jigsaw that she'd half forgotten she was even doing.

She concocted a response along the same breezy lines and told herself there was absolutely nothing wrong in getting back in touch. He was just an old friend. And maybe he'd know someone interested in renting the villa. Even so, her finger hesitated a fraction of a minute before pressing the 'send' button on her computer.

So much can hinge on a few seconds of indecision. So much hovers uncertainly in the balance. So much to be gained, and so much to be lost.

From that moment on, Susan checked her emails compulsively, all the while trying to play down any feelings of excitement. Nevertheless, when his name finally popped up again in her inbox, she couldn't help noticing how her stomach seemed to be fluttering, and she gazed at the bold letters in shock for a few moments before double-clicking on his message.

As she'd predicted, he was married. He told her about his life in the RAF, stationed at Lyneham in Wiltshire and about his two children. She replied, describing a bit about meeting Franco and moving to Sardinia. Before long they were in regular contact and the more they communicated, the closer they became.

With Franco there was often a barrier of some sort – whether it was language, or cultural understanding or different backgrounds, she couldn't say. But with Steve, there was nothing in the way. Each knew where the other came from. They knew each other's families. They'd grown up among the same people, against the same backdrop. They even shared the same memories. They could talk to each other about anything and everything.

It wasn't long before emailing Steve became the highlight of Susan's day. There's nothing wrong with it, she'd tell herself. We're just friends. To Franco, she let on that she was back in contact with old school pals, and he was hopeful that strengthening her connections with home would make her feel less isolated in Sardinia. But even while she was convincing herself they were just a couple of old mates who'd found each other again, Susan was beginning to realise deep down that this was something more. Even over the Internet, the connection between them was so powerful, it was almost as if he was reading her thoughts. They seemed to be of the same mind about almost everything, and barely an email went past without one or other of them pointing out some bizarre similarity or coincidence.

After a few months with emails flying to and fro between them, it became impossible to ignore what was happening. Without meaning to, or wanting to, the two reunited childhood sweethearts had fallen back in love. Within months they'd graduated from emails to Instant Messenger – the cyber equivalent of chatting in real time.

While Franco remained unaware of how intense the

friendship had become, Stephen's wife, Doreen, became suspicious, once phoning Susan to tell her effectively to back off. But by that time it was too late. Susan and Stephen were already too involved to be torn apart a second time.

Although it was already pretty obvious from his communications, Steve blurted out his feelings in a phone call from the States. 'I love you,' he told a trembling Susan. 'I want to spend the rest of my life with you.'

It wasn't what either would have chosen to happen, but now that it had happened, they found they just couldn't go back to how things were. Inevitably, the two started to make plans to meet. They had to know whether this thing was real, or whether they'd just constructed a nostalgic fantasy that would crumble to dust when confronted by their actual middle-aged selves.

In February 2006, Susan arranged a visit back to the UK. The night before the meeting she'd organised with Stephen she was so nervous she could hardly sleep. The last time they'd met, she'd been a teenager; now she was 52 years old. What if he was horrified by how much she'd changed? Part of her almost hoped the meeting would be a disaster and they could each go back to their lives without hurting anyone, but another part knew that losing Stephen all over again would leave a gaping hole in her soul that would be impossible to fill.

In the event, she need not have worried. After the initial shock of having to readjust to the changes more than three decades had wrought on their appearances, it was as if those changes began to dissolve away as soon as they began speaking. Just a short time together and they were once again the Sue and Steve they'd been at school, when the future had stretched out in front of them like a glittering prize and anything had seemed possible.

That night they lay together in an anonymous hotel room, just holding each other, creating just for a few precious hours, a safe cocoon around themselves in which nothing else existed but the two of them.

By the time Susan returned to Sardinia, she knew she was in effect going back to say goodbye. How many times during that long flight back did she wish she could rewind time, so that she and Stephen would have stayed together and no one else would have to suffer? How often did she picture the hurt in Franco's eyes when she told him, or think of the pain she was about to inflict on Stephen's wife – a woman she didn't even know? And yet how could she bear to throw away a second chance at happiness?

Between February and April of 2006, Susan carried her secret around with her like a ticking bomb. So many times she thought about coming clean to Franco, but she could never find the right words. And after all, is there ever a 'right' way to ruin a man's life? Is there a magical combination of words that can stop a heart from breaking?

And besides, Susan was slightly concerned about Franco's emotional unpredictability. Not that he'd ever shown any signs of violence – far from it – but he loved her so much, there was no telling how the news could affect him. What if he flew off the handle? What if he tried to stop her from leaving the island? She had no transport of her own, no way of getting around without him – and if he took away her passport, in effect she'd be a prisoner.

Over in England, a heavy-hearted Stephen set about the soul-destroying task of dismantling a marriage, detonating a grenade through the lives of an unsuspecting family, but in Sardinia, Susan kept her counsel. She'd decided she couldn't risk breaking the news to Franco face to face. She'd write him a letter when she returned to England explaining everything and begging for his understanding. She knew it was a cowardly way of ending things, but she believed it was the only way she could be sure of saying what needed to be said, without having to fear how he'd react.

In April, she booked another flight back to the UK, ostensibly to attend a party to celebrate her son's birthday. The night before she left, she was assailed by so many different emotions – excitement, dread, guilt, pity – all pulling her in different directions. 'It'll be all right in the end,' she kept trying to reassure herself.

Hopefully, in a few years time they'd all have moved on and this would all be just a painful memory.

She and Franco had both weathered marriage break-ups before and gone on to love again. It was horrible, but it was life. That night she made love to Franco one last time. Was it a parting gift, or a way of assuaging a guilty conscience? Or was it more prosaic than that – a way of ensuring he didn't suspect anything was amiss? Most likely it was a combination of all three. Human relationships are made up of more layers than an onion, each one paper thin, and transparently fragile. And when you slice them open, they don't come apart cleanly but crumble into so many pieces you wonder how they'd ever been whole to start with.

Back in the UK, she and Stephen met up again, with the initial shyness of the teenagers they'd once been. They'd both committed everything to being together. There could be no going back. Stephen – who'd always prided himself on living honourably, both in his private life and in the RAF, where he had a reputation as a nice guy and a true gentleman – was still reeling from the devastation he'd caused to his family. Susan was tied up in knots about the bombshell she had yet to drop on hers. At last she could put it off no longer, and made the phone call she'd been dreading.

✳   ✳   ✳

In Sardinia, Franco Matta gripped onto the receiver in an attempt to anchor himself to reality as the world seemed to slide from under his feet.

What was Susan talking about? It was just days before that he'd left her at the airport, telling her he'd be there to pick her up when she returned. How could she now be saying she wasn't coming back?

'I'm so sorry,' she kept repeating, uselessly. 'I'm so sorry.'

Still his brain couldn't process what it was hearing. She was telling him she couldn't live in Sardinia any longer, that the marriage was over, although she desperately didn't want to hurt him. There'd be a letter explaining everything.

Strange, how in the course of one phone call the whole world can change, the colours of a beautiful spring Sardinian day becoming slightly muted, the noises of the waves no longer so reassuring. Franco had truly thought that in Susan, he'd found his life's partner. Without her, what was his life? A hollow thing, with an empty space at its core.

After he put the phone down, the silence was more than he could bear. Whereas just a few minutes before, he'd revelled in his solitude, knowing it would make him appreciate Susan's company even more when she returned, suddenly he felt weighed down by an oppressive loneliness such as he'd never felt before. And still he couldn't understand what she'd been telling him. Since when had she been so unhappy here? Since when had she been so discontented with him? Surely there was nothing they couldn't put right if they worked on it together? Why hadn't she given him a chance to change?

Susan had told him she was sending him a letter explaining everything. The days he spent waiting for it to arrive passed agonisingly slowly while every single scenario and outcome passed through his fevered imagination. There were moments of hope when he convinced himself she was just reacting to being back on home turf, surrounded by friends and family and that she'd soon change her mind once the novelty had worn off. Then, minutes later, he'd be plunged into despair, remembering how she'd sounded so final on the phone, as though nothing he could say would change her mind.

When the letter eventually arrived, he gazed at it a long time, his eyes caressing the writing he knew so well, drawing comfort just from knowing it was her hand that formed the letters. Ridiculous how running his fingertips across the ink made him feel somehow connected to her. But as he read the words Susan had so carefully composed, any last vestiges of hope or optimism he had been clinging to over the last days drained slowly away.

There was another man, she revealed, someone from her past with whom she had a strong bond, and with whom she might have a future. She'd been missing England and she wanted to stay there. The marriage was over. *I hope you will not hate me,* she pleaded. *I cannot help my feelings. I can no longer be your wife.* The letter ended: *Please stay calm and don't do anything that could put you in harm's way. You are a good man. This is not your fault. It's mine. Sue x*

With each word, Franco felt as though his insides were being ripped out through his throat, leaving them exposed, pulped and raw. His legs were shaking and the words on the paper seemed blurred and nonsensical.

Another man.

The phrase went round and round in his brain like the insistent whine of a mosquito, impossible to ignore. Another man. Another man.

As a lover, he was heartbroken. As a husband, he was betrayed. And as a Sardinian, he was humiliated.

There was another man. His wife had left him. She was never coming home.

※　※　※

In England, Susan was torn between relief at having unburdened herself finally, and guilt at how wretched she had made her husband who had done nothing wrong, except perhaps to love too much.

She was already dreading going back to Sardinia to pick up her things. How could she look Franco in the eyes, knowing the hurt she'd find there – hurt that she alone had caused? How could she face their friends? Wouldn't they all think she was turning her back on them?

And yet, agonising though it was, she knew it felt right to be with Stephen. There was a bond so strong there, it made all of this emotional turbulence bearable. They began house-hunting, looking for a place in which they'd be free to get to know one another again, and from which they could begin to renegotiate their place in the world.

They soon found a house in a small, brand-new development in a quiet, leafy part of Tiverton. It wasn't showy, but it was unfussy and secluded. Plus, there's something about new developments that makes you feel optimistic, as though everyone is starting again from scratch, almost with a clean slate. New houses carry no baggage, no ghosts, no memories. New neighbours know no secrets.

With the deposit paid, there was nothing left but to look forward to moving in, but still Susan's happiness was clouded by the prospect of facing Franco again. From the texts he'd been sending her, telling her how much he loved her, how much he missed her, she knew he hadn't even begun to accept that the relationship was over and she couldn't bear the idea of having to go over it with him face to face, breaking his heart all over again. Yet she knew she had to get it over with.

With a heavy heart, she booked her flight back.

✳   ✳   ✳

In Sardinia, the news of Susan's imminent arrival sent Franco into a tailspin. He'd read and re-read the letter she'd sent a thousand times, but still he persuaded himself there must be some glimmer of hope. She was coming back, which meant she'd be able to see for herself just how much he loved her. In person, they'd be able to talk properly about what they could do to make her feel more at home on the island. If only she'd told him when she first started feeling homesick, they could have averted all this heartache.

Looking around him at the pine trees rustling gently in the warm breeze and the sunlight sparkling like Christmas tinsel on the distant sea, he told himself that Susan wouldn't be able to help being seduced by the island all over again when she arrived fresh from hemmed-in, cloud-dampened Devon.

He had another chance to win her over and he was determined not to fail. He had to think of a gesture to show her he understood how she'd been feeling, something to give her life in Sardinia focus and make her feel connected to the island once again. And then it came to him, a sudden inspiration, something he was sure she wouldn't be able to resist.

✳   ✳   ✳

As she made her way through to the arrivals lounge at Cagliari Elmas airport, Susan's heart was thudding so loudly she was surprised the other passengers couldn't hear it. What state would Franco be in? Would he be angry – who could blame him if he was? Or, worse, would he be in pieces waiting to meet her, a shadow of the man he'd been?

Of all the scenarios that passed through Susan's anguished mind, none prepared her for walking through customs to find Franco waiting for her, a big smile bursting out all over his face and clutching in his arms… a puppy.

'It's for you!' he told her, proffering the wriggling little creature eagerly.

A puppy! What was he thinking of? All through the drive back to the house, Susan asked herself how he could have got it so terribly, catastrophically wrong. To think you could use a pet to paper over the cracks in a marriage. To believe a dog could take the place of a soul mate… She realised during the short journey home that Franco really hadn't understood at all what she'd tried to tell him in the letter and, with a sinking feeling, she understood she would have to go through it all over again.

It was a very different Franco who said goodbye to his beloved Susan before her return flight a couple of days later. Gone was the big smile, the hopeful optimism that, after all, love could conquer everything. Gone was the quiet conviction that if he could just show his wife what was in his heart, she'd agree to stay, to give their marriage another chance. In its place was a broken man, already deflating around the empty space that had suddenly opened up inside of him.

✳   ✳   ✳

With the long-dreaded trip to Sardinia over, moving into the house in Tidcombe Walk at the end of June 2006, felt truly like a new beginning.

Can there be anything more pleasingly symbolic than pooling possessions with a partner you intend to spend the rest of your life with, deciding what photo to put where, exclaiming over identical books or CDs?

If only Franco could accept it was over, Susan thought, she might be completely happy, but he continued sending her messages, telling her how much he missed her. Each time she saw his name pop up on her phone, Susan's heart constricted, as though someone had given it a sudden squeeze.

She hadn't told him that she was moving in with Stephen – it seemed like rubbing salt in the wound – but he nevertheless tracked down her new address. She groaned when a postcard arrived and she realised it was from him. *I cannot stop thinking about you,* it read. *You are the blood in my veins.*

On 2 July, Susan spoke to her estranged husband on

the phone while he was staying in Switzerland. At this stage he still had no idea just how involved she was with her old flame, let alone that she had set up house with him. But something in her conversation, something in her voice, gave the game away.

When Franco came off the phone, it was as though something inside him, something that had been stretching tighter and tighter over the past weeks since Susan's bombshell, snapped completely. And when it snapped, so did all sense of who he was and how he should live his life. He just had one thought in his head. To find Susan.

❊   ❊   ❊

It was early in the evening on 6 July when Franco's hired van pulled up outside Susan and Stephen's new house. The sun was still hovering uncertainly in the sky as he raised his hand to ring the doorbell, and the sound of distant children's excited screaming mingled with the scent of freshly mown lawns in air that seemed swollen with the promise of summer.

When Susan and Stephen opened the door of their new home to find Franco Matta standing there, there was a moment of sheer shock followed by a sense of inevitability. It was not a visit either would have wished for, but now he was here, they felt they had better get the meeting over with, then maybe they could all attempt to move on with their lives. And at least the Sardinian appeared to be calm and in control.

Once inside, however, it became obvious that despite Franco's initially calm demeanour this was no social call. 'I thought you were an officer and a gentleman,' he told Stephen angrily as he was shown into the living room.

Steve and Susan exchanged a nervous look, but their resolve was absolute.

'You have to accept this,' Stephen told him, patiently and coolly. 'Nothing is going to change.'

Without any alteration to his uncharacteristic, cold behaviour, Franco started telling them that he'd hired a mafia hitman to do away with Steve, and they'd need to pay 50,000 euros to call him off. That was too much for Stephen. He'd spent his entire adult life in the forces, and he wasn't about to let someone stand in his living room threatening him with the Mob.

'I'm calling the police,' he said. 'I'm not going to live in fear.'

And that was when it happened. Susan could only watch in horror as a cold, hard monster that seemed to have taken the place of her normally loving, warm-hearted Sardinian husband, lunged at her new lover as he sat in an armchair.

Something glinted in his hand. Metallic silver.

'Sue, he has a knife,' Steve cried out, but seconds later that fact became all too obvious as blood started to pump out from the deep wounds in his neck and throat.

Shouting out for Franco to stop, Susan called 999 and then dashed from the room to grab a towel to staunch the blood, which by now appeared to be everywhere. Her heart was hammering so hard she couldn't breathe. *My God, my God, my God, this cannot be real...*

Having snatched up the first towel to hand, she raced back into the living room and bent down towards Stephen, cradling his head in her arms, trying to stop the bleeding. But it was already too late.

Franco was watching blankly.

'My life is over,' he told her. 'Now you will suffer as I am suffering.'

Picking up the phone, Franco called his brother Aldo, who was working in London and with whom he had stayed on the way to Devon. 'The thing I thought wasn't going to happen has happened,' he told him, in a voice as devoid of feeling as his expression.

By the time police arrived, Franco was once again calm and docile, despite his own injuries sustained in the scuffle with Steve. But he was still a million miles from the Franco that Susan had married and loved and who'd worshipped the ground she walked on. This Franco stared at her with eyes like empty wells.

'I came here to kill the man,' he told police, levelly. 'I have done what I had to do. I have done my job. I am an executioner.'

Then he turned his impassive gaze to Susan.

'I love you,' he told her as he was led away.

'Shut up!' The words were ripped painfully from her throat, as she held her lifeless lover in her arms. 'Don't talk to me.'

❋   ❋   ❋

In October 2007, Francesco Matta was tried for murder at Exeter Crown Court but pleaded not guilty. The jury heard that though he accepted he had killed Stephen Keen, he maintained he should be convicted of manslaughter on the grounds of diminished responsibility. After several days of deliberation the jury failed to reach a majority verdict and a retrial was ordered.

Finally, on 18 April 2008, after a second trial, Francesco Matta was found guilty of murdering Stephen Keen, and was told he would serve at least 13 years and six months for the crime.

As the broken man was led away to begin his sentence, and Susan Matta and Stephen Keen's family prepared to start trying to piece together a life without the man they'd all loved so much, it was clear there were no winners at this bleakest of trials. 'If there is something romantic in the way people who had once been in love found each other after so many years, the event was also the beginning of a tragedy,' prosecutor Martin Meeke commented during the court proceedings.

FRIENDS AGAIN...

When past and present collide, everyone around is caught up in the blast and nothing, afterwards, looks quite the same again.

CHAPTER THREE
YOU CAN'T HURRY LOVE

hewing anxiously on the edge of his finger, James Beresford-Wylie tried in vain to talk himself out of being so nervous. It was just a school reunion, he told himself sternly, a chance to meet up with a bunch of old mates. And yes, it would be great if something happened at last with Jane, but he wasn't going to get too worked up about it. He'd just see how things went; go with the flow.

James was full of good intentions, which lasted... well, right up until the point when Jane walked into the room. After that, all theories about not raising his hopes and not having unrealistic expectations went right out of the window. Eighteen years after they'd gone out together at school, and she was still his ideal woman. Everything about her, from her dark-brown hair to her beautiful smile, made him melt inside.

What a good idea it had been to help organise this reunion, tying it in with Jane coming over from Australia, where she'd been living. The Friends Reunited website hadn't been going very long, but he could already see how, with so many people like him still carrying secret torches for long-lost loves, it would be a mammoth success. He just had to be careful not to blow it. Now, after all this time, it was surely his chance.

But life has a funny habit of not doing what you want it to. Although the reunion put James back in touch with the girl of his dreams, and the stage was set for riding off into the sunset, the path of true love was about to prove about as smooth as... sandpaper.

* * *

It's never easy moving to a new school when you're a kid, particularly when everyone else already knows each other. James Beresford-Wylie was 12 when his family moved from Wantage to Yate, in Avon, and starting Brimsham Green School was a bit of an ordeal. So focused was he on trying to make friends with the other boys and fit in, that he didn't really pay much attention to the girls in his class. Then one day, when he'd been at the school about a year, a note was passed to him in Music.

'Do you want to go out with Jane?' it asked, in typically blunt teenage fashion.

James was thrilled. He'd never even thought about

approaching Jane, who always seemed so much older and more mature than him and all his gang. Still, he was hardly going to say 'no', was he? He hastily scrawled 'yes' on the note and handed it back.

Jane, for her part, had noticed James almost as soon as he arrived at the school – he was tall, with amazing blue eyes. Even though her best friend had told her she'd be mad to go out with someone with curly hair, she hadn't been put off. Deciding she was bored with waiting for him to make a move, she'd taken the matter into her own hands.

So, in this singularly unromantic fashion, James and Jane became boyfriend and girlfriend – although, like most 13-year-olds, they had little idea of what this actually entailed.

Every day, James would walk her home from school to the other side of town, wheeling his BMX, and they'd stop at the Kiosks newsagents in town where Jane would buy him a little chocolate elephant for his trouble. Then, having deposited her safely home, he'd ride the three or four miles back to his own house on the other side of town.

You might think they'd have lots of time for in-depth, soul-bearing talks during these long walks, but in fact, like many kids their age, they steered well clear of anything remotely meaningful. In reality, they were both going through similar unhappy situations at home with parents breaking up, but as they avoided personal subjects like the plague, neither had any idea of the other's secret heartache.

Every now and then, they'd break off from their mostly silent trudging to have a kiss – once looking up to find an entire factory floor standing at the window laughing at them – but in truth, it was far from the romance of the century. They were at that self-centred stage in life where everyone else is just a bit player in the central drama, which, of course, is themselves. Inevitably, they drifted apart and even their break-up was a bit of a non-event – no tears, no regrets or recriminations. One day, James rode his bike straight home after school instead of waiting for a by this time largely indifferent Jane – and that was the end of that.

Shortly afterwards, James's father moved to Wickwar, about nine miles away from Yate and James, reluctantly went to live with him, changing schools yet again. For five years he didn't see Jane, and though he thought about her from time to time, as a teenager with no transport of his own, he knew there was little hope of meeting up with her again.

It wasn't until he was 18 that James started going back to Yate. By this time he'd become a Goth and there was a nightclub there called Spirals that ran a good night every Tuesday, with music that appealed to his selective tastes. One Tuesday night, he was sitting in Spirals with his mates when the door opened and a glamorous brunette walked in. Jane.

'Oh my God, I know her,' he muttered to his friends as this gorgeous apparition drew closer, having clearly recognised him.

'It's James, isn't it?' she said. And then she was sitting down at his table and they talked and talked, in a way they'd been quite unable to do five years before.

Jane told James all about the guy she was seeing and how she didn't know if he was right for her. James nodded in all the right places, but inside he was thinking, *She looks so fantastic. Why am I still such a little twerp?*

He wondered whether he had the nerve to ask for her number, but then just as the club was about to close, she jumped up and said: 'I've got to go. See you.'

And she was gone.

Far from the casual nonchalance with which he'd greeted their break-up five years before, James was thrown into a state of near upheaval by Jane's sudden reappearance into his life – and her subsequent disappearance. For the whole of that week he thought about her and how lovely she'd looked, but he was convinced he wouldn't see her again. So when, the following Tuesday, he looked up from his usual table in Spirals to see Jane walking towards him, a broad smile on her face, he was elated.

'She must have come back to see me,' he told himself incredulously.

Once again, they talked all night, and once again Jane was complaining about her current partner. But the more she talked, the more James convinced himself that he'd got it wrong. She couldn't be interested in him. She was so sophisticated, so gorgeous. What could she possibly see in someone like him?

'Do you want a lift home, then?' Jane was standing with her friend, looking at him expectantly.

James was flustered. 'Er, no, you're all right. I'll go back with my mates,' he stammered.

Immediately he felt a sharp dig in his side, where his friend had prodded him. 'No you're not,' his mate hissed, staring pointedly at him. 'You'd love a lift, wouldn't you?'

And so James found himself trying to cram his six-foot-three frame into the back seat of Jane's tiny green Mini, with her girlfriend in the front seat, obviously finding the situation vastly amusing.

As they drew up outside his house, after dropping off the friend, James unfolded his aching limbs and clambered painfully out of the car. For a while, he and Jane stood outside chatting nervously, before the cold caused them to move back inside the front of the car again. Once again Jane was making a great show of complaining about her boyfriend, saying that he didn't appreciate her. As far as she was concerned, she was signalling her interest as blatantly as she could, without actually asking him out herself.

James knew he should ask for her number, and yet he just couldn't articulate the words. What if he'd misread the signs? Wouldn't it be embarrassing if she didn't feel that way about him at all? In the end, he convinced himself he was better off waiting until the following Tuesday night. With all the background noise and people around, it'd be a lot less embarrassing than standing awkwardly by the Mini.

As she drove off, he was already imagining what he'd say to her the next time they met. How he'd be a hundred times more suave and confident. He had no idea, as the tail-lights of the little Mini disappeared around the corner, that he wouldn't see her again for 13 years.

When Jane didn't turn up at Spirals the following Tuesday, James was crest-fallen. Every time the door opened, he felt a surge of hope, followed by a thud of disappointment as it turned out not to be her. When the night passed without Jane showing up, he started asking around, to see if anyone knew where she might live, but he met with a resounding blank.

For weeks and months after that, he looked for her whenever he was in the area, but with a decreasing degree of optimism. He'd moved away from home to a bedsit, which made him feel lonely and miserable, and only made him think of Jane more and wish he could find her again.

Eventually, he found someone who knew where she was. But the news wasn't good. She'd gone to live in Australia with a guy called Mike she'd worked with back in England.

It was all over before it had even begun.

For Jane, moving to Australia made perfect sense. She'd liked James and tried to make something happen between them. She'd thought she was being as obvious as she possibly could be that time she turned up at Spirals and offered him a lift home. What more could she have done? So when he hadn't picked up the initiative and asked for her number, she'd given up. He obviously wasn't that keen. And she wasn't about to lose any more sleep over it. When the chance had come up to work in Australia, she'd thought, *Why not?* After all, there was nothing to hold her back.

James, left behind in a town that suddenly seemed so much emptier and greyer without Jane, was devastated. So that was it, he berated himself. He'd blown it. He was plunged into depression, but he knew there was little point moping about. He'd had his chance and now she was gone.

Little by little he forced himself to forget about Jane and the perfect romance that had, as he belatedly realised, only ever existed in his head, and focus on finding a real woman with whom to start a real relationship.

By the time James heard that Jane and Mike had got married in Australia, in 1988, he was also involved with someone else, so the news didn't carry quite such a punch as it might otherwise have done. While he still thought of Jane from time to time, he'd managed to file her away in the back of his head, like a bag of outgrown clothes pushed to the back of the wardrobe. That same year, in an unintentional twist of fate, James also got married.

Unfortunately for James, married life wasn't quite all he'd imagined. The meeting of minds he'd blithely assumed marriage to be never quite materialised. As the years went by, it became increasingly obvious he'd made a mistake and by 1998 he was divorced and single again.

Over the years, he never completely forgot about Jane. But no one seemed to have any more news about her and he was sure she was still in Australia and happily married, so there seemed little point in even attempting to get in touch with her.

In due course, James met somebody else and, ignoring the little warning voice inside him telling him it wasn't right, he hurled himself headlong into another unsatisfactory relationship.

It was 2000 when a friend from Yate days got in touch to talk about a new website that had been launched to put old school friends back in touch. Wouldn't it be fun to organise a reunion?

James agreed. From his vantage point as an adult whose romantic and professional life had so far spectacularly failed to live up to the expectations of his youth, returning to the past seemed like a welcome relief. Between them, the two friends set about contacting all their old classmates who'd signed up to the site. One of them was Jane.

When James first saw the familiar name on the class list, he felt a shock of excitement as surprise, pleasure and regret, all rushed through him in one giddy cocktail of emotion. But he quickly got himself under control. From her profile it was obvious she was still in Oz and still married. He knew he had to be realistic.

When he sent her a friendly email telling her about the reunion, she replied fairly immediately, explaining that if they could tie it in with her forthcoming visit to the UK she'd be delighted to attend. Oh, and the timing couldn't be better as she'd just got divorced.

Divorced? And yet still James told himself not to get too excited. The truth was she still lived on the other side of the world, and he was with somebody else. It would be lovely to see her, he rationalised, but just as friends.

A couple of days before the reunion was scheduled, James was halfway through a shift at the printing firm where he worked nights, when his mobile phone rang. It was Jane.

'I'm here,' she announced cheerfully, her voice instantly transporting him back 13 years. 'Want to meet up before we face everyone else?'

Immediately all his big ideas about being realistic and not allowing himself to get carried away went right out of the window. They arranged to meet for lunch the following day, and James spent the whole of that night constructing fantasies in his head, which he then angrily tried to wipe from his mind.

Stuck in a miserable relationship, he couldn't help hoping that Jane was going to be the answer to his problems – that she'd walk through the door and it'd be love at first sight and everything would be easy. Overnight, he rewrote their history into a romance of epic proportions in which separation and loss are finally overcome by the redemptive power of love. Sadly, outside of Hollywood, life doesn't work like that.

When Jane came into the restaurant the following day, 13 years after driving away from him in her Mini, she didn't fling herself into his arms, or throw him a look that said: 'How foolish we've been. We're made for each other.' Nor was he instantly struck by the realisation that here was his ideal woman. Instead, his first thought was, *Blimey, she's skinny*.

With all the stress of the divorce, plus a newly

discovered passion for running, Jane had lost a lot of weight and while she was rejoicing in her new slim-line physique, James couldn't help thinking he'd preferred her when she was a little more curvy. Plus, she didn't exactly come over as someone who'd been hit over the head by a thunderbolt of love upon seeing him. Rather she was bright and breezy and friendly, just as if he was any old mate. Which, he supposed, he was.

Nevertheless, lunch was a great success, and the two former childhood sweethearts talked and talked, just as they had in Spirals all those years ago. By the end, James was hoping for a kiss and was disappointed when Jane turned to him and said lightly, 'Oh, I won't kiss you as you're in a relationship,' before running off.

Still, there was the reunion the next night. The more James thought about it, the more convinced he became that this was when something was finally going to happen between him and Jane. Sure, she'd been a bit casual at lunchtime, but then she'd just come out of a divorce, she wasn't about to start getting heavy with the first guy she had lunch with. But tomorrow night would be a different story, he was sure of it. Deliberately ignoring the fact that he was involved with someone else – which ought, by rights, to rule out any romantic daydreams – he lost himself in fantasies about what the coming day would bring. Tomorrow he'd make her see how much he'd grown up in the last 13 years, he decided, and how good they'd be together.

The night of the reunion, James took special care over getting ready. He knew Jane was flying back soon after and it was his last chance to impress her. He was so nervous he felt once again like the schoolboy he'd been when they first met.

At the reunion, he kept an anxious eye on the door, refilling his drink more frequently than was probably wise in an attempt to steady his racing nerves. When he saw her come in, looking incredible in a dress that showed off her running-toned figure, he was shocked at the ferocity of his happiness at seeing her again. This time, nothing was going to stop him telling her how he felt.

Well, nothing except maybe the fact she'd arranged to meet another ex-boyfriend there... only she'd sort of neglected to mention that to James.

Jane clocked the fleeting look of hurt surprise that came over James's face, but decided to ignore it. After 12 years of marriage, she was enjoying the feeling of giddy liberation that came with being single and being back in her childhood home. And to be honest, she didn't really think James took her terribly seriously anyway, so why shouldn't she invite her old beau and have some fun?

James, for his part, made a decision that, ex-boyfriend or no ex-boyfriend, he wasn't going to let

Jane get away again without letting her know how he felt. The evening was imbued with a kind of magical fatalism, he decided. There was a sense of destiny about it. Everything pointed towards this being the night he finally got his girl.

But when the end of the night came, Jane had disappeared. James looked for her everywhere. At first he wasn't too concerned – she'd be getting her coat, or swapping numbers with an old friend. But with every minute that passed, he grew increasingly anxious. By now, the venue had largely cleared and there was still no sign of her.

Eventually, he discovered what had happened.

'Oh, Jane left with that guy she used to go out with,' someone told him cheerily.

Immediately, it was as if something fundamental shifted in the world around him. The venue, which had previously seemed like the backdrop to a film set, was suddenly revealed to be just another smoke-ridden bar, the lights were too bright, the furnishings shabby. If the ceiling tiles had fallen in on his head at that moment, James couldn't have felt in more pain. Yet again all his hopes, all his expectations, had come to nothing. Yet again the girl of his dreams had vanished, turning all his fantasies to dust that slipped through his fingers.

When his best friend Dominic came to find him, James couldn't hide the state he was in. 'You've just got to forget about her, mate,' Dominic told him. 'She's not worth it.'

But something inside told James she *was* worth it. And, as anyone who's ever been through an agonising break up or rejection will attest, it's no use hearing about how many more fish there are in the sea when you've got your heart set on one particular minnow.

James was inconsolable. That night he slunk dejectedly back to the flat he shared with his girlfriend. His feelings for Jane over the last 48 hours had brought home to him exactly what was lacking in his relationship, and how unhealthy it had become, yet he felt too emotionally battered to think about anything else apart from just getting through the next few days. Gradually, life slipped back into the same unsatisfying rut it had inhabited before his meeting with Jane had thrown it momentarily into such sharp relief.

Strangely, although the reunion ended so badly, at least as far as James was concerned, it seemed to signify the start of a new phase in his and Jane's relationship. Once back in Australia, Jane emailed James regularly, telling him all about what was happening in her life. She knew he was unhappy in his relationship and constantly urged him to get out of it. Conversely, when she met someone new who, it was immediately obvious, wasn't right for her, James also tried to persuade her to cut her losses and leave.

Over the next six years, as both continued to limp along in their increasingly unsatisfying relationships, they fashioned themselves into a mutual support system for one another. If James was unhappy, Jane was the person he poured his heart out to. Similarly, when Jane was feeling trapped, it was James she turned to. 'If only you were here,' they'd tell each other regularly. 'You need looking after properly.'

In the meantime, back in the real world, James was reaching a crisis point in his life. In 2006, the printing factory where he worked as production manager closed down and he was offered a year's contract at a printing company in Edinburgh. It would mean living on his own in a flat near the city and flying down to Avon for the odd weekend.

For James, who'd always dreaded being on his own, it was a revelation. Far from hating single life, he found it such a relief to come home from work at the end of the day and relax, knowing there would be no tension or arguments. He enjoyed not having to compromise all the time, or to worry about someone else's moods or whims. After a couple of months, he realised with a shock that he would be OK living on his own. In fact, he'd be fine.

And yet, still he couldn't seem to bring himself to end his relationship. As 2006 wore on, James continued his commuting lifestyle, flying down to see his girlfriend most weekends. Meanwhile, the emails between him and

Jane carried on as usual. Seeing her name pop up in his inbox when he logged onto the computer at work was the highlight of his day. No matter how long it had been since they'd last seen each other, there was still something so special about her. She seemed to understand him in a way even friends he saw all the time often didn't.

Jane wrote about her job, working as a sales rep for a publishing company. And she told him about her new friend who lived in the flat above her. 'Come over and see me,' she wrote to him, not completely in jest. 'You can meet Caroline and then you'll have a blonde AND a brunette.'

James was due to get redundancy pay at the end of that year and his friends, knowing how destructive his relationship had become and bored at the way so many of his sentences seemed to start 'Jane says...', were constantly urging him to ditch his partner and use the money to fly off to Australia to win Jane over.

Although at first he laughed off the idea, James couldn't help coming back to it again and again. Was it really so ridiculous? At least that way he'd know he'd tried, and he wouldn't have to live the rest of his life with the niggling doubt that he'd let the love of his life get away. Again.

But before he could come to any decisions, Jane sent him an email that changed everything. She'd decided to get married to the guy she was seeing, in a last-ditch attempt to save their disintegrating relationship.

In vain did James tell her she was making a mistake – she was determined to go through with it. She'd invested so many years in this relationship, she couldn't bear the idea of walking away with nothing yet again.

Alone in his Edinburgh flat, James raged about the unfairness of everything and the uselessness of their timing. Just when he was getting the emotional strength together to exit his relationship, Jane was about to irretrievably commit to hers. It was all so twisted and wrong, but it didn't seem that there was anything he could do about it.

In the end, he didn't have to. The next email he received from Jane, in September 2006, conveyed a complete change in tone. Her boyfriend had developed cold feet about getting married. He wanted to stay together, but not to take the big step. Jane was hurt and upset. She needed to get away and think everything through. She was flying over to the UK. Could she come to visit?

James couldn't believe it. You know how sometimes when you want something so much and you finally get it, you're left with a kind of emptiness where that wanting used to be? Suddenly he felt scared and excited and empty and jubilant, all at the same time.

Over the next few weeks, Jane finalised her travel

plans. She was flying into London on 2 November and would go from there to see her family in Avon, then she'd fly up to see James in Edinburgh on the following Monday, staying until Wednesday, and then back to Oz the weekend after.

As the date grew nearer, James grew increasingly nervous. There was so much riding on this one flying visit. A whole lifetime of hopes and fantasies and regrets hung in the balance. How many more chances would he get? He had to seize this one.

But at the same time there was that underlying fear that maybe he was just setting himself up for disappointment one more time. Jane was escaping from rejection in Australia. She wouldn't be looking for anything romantic. She just saw him as a friend. The doubts weren't assuaged by his friend Dominic coming up to see him a few days before Jane's visit to implore him not to get involved.

'Remember how cut up you were that night of the reunion?' Dominic warned him. 'You're just going to get hurt all over again. Sleep with her if you have to, but whatever you do don't go falling in love.'

The Friday before Jane was due to arrive in Edinburgh, James flew down to Bristol as usual to see his girlfriend. It was a very surreal weekend. He knew what he was doing wasn't right, and that he should have the guts to follow his heart and tell her it was all over.

But somehow he just couldn't articulate the words. By this time their relationship had become so twisted and toxic that they'd both lost the ability to talk honestly and hid instead behind long-established routines, and old simmering resentments.

Monday morning, James was up at 3.45am to get the plane from Bristol to Edinburgh. Even at this early hour, his excitement was at fever pitch. He couldn't believe that by the end of the day, he and Jane would be together. His fantasy woman was about to become flesh and blood. Nipping into a shop on the way back to his flat, he filled a shopping basket with things he knew she liked – Revels, certain types of cheese. He wanted to make sure the kitchen was stocked with stuff that she'd missed while she was in Australia.

As soon as he got into work, he logged onto the computer and called up two screens, one showing live departures from Stansted and the other live arrivals at Edinburgh. He was due to be back at the airport meeting Jane's plane at 1pm, and he wanted to track its journey up from London.

The plane information from Stansted was satisfyingly detailed. He followed her flight's progress as the boarding gate was announced, then last call. Then finally it was taxiing and then... nothing. Each time James was called away from his desk, he'd come back to find Jane's flight was still on the tarmac. He couldn't believe it. After all this time, the plane had broken down.

All his careful timetabling of when he'd have to leave to get to the airport on time went out of the window as he watched the screen. Minutes went by, then hours, and still it was taxiing.

As the clock ticked on past 1pm, James could feel all his earlier joyous anticipation draining away. Unable to stay at his desk a moment longer, he went off to meet with his HR manager. When he came back to his desk ten minutes later, the screen had changed. Next to Jane's flight, where just a short while before had been the information that the plane was still taxiing on the tarmac, was just one word: 'Landed.'

For a few seconds, all James could do was stare at the screen uncomprehendingly. Then it hit him. There'd been a malfunction. While the screen had been showing Jane's plane as being stuck on the tarmac, it had actually been winging its way serenely northwards and had already landed at Edinburgh. Jane would at this moment be walking through Customs and scanning the crowd for his face.

Cursing under his breath, he flew out of the building and jumped into his car, speeding over to the airport as quickly as he could. Even so, it was 1.45pm when he eventually emerged, red-faced and panting, into the arrivals hall at Edinburgh airport.

'Please let her still be there,' he muttered under his breath. 'Please let me not be too late.'

He looked everywhere – the expectant crowd clustered by the arrivals door, the knots of people standing around the sidelines. But she was nowhere to be seen. Then, just as he was beginning to think he'd blown it yet again, there was a voice behind him.

'Wylie.'

And there she was.

In life there are very few moments that come close to emulating the way things happen in the movies. But this was one of them. In that split second after turning round, James knew without a shadow of a doubt that this was it – she was the one. Without even stopping to think, he swept Jane up in his arms, lifting her off the floor in a Hollywood-style embrace.

Much later, Jane would admit that when she'd got off the plane and found he wasn't there, she'd at first thought he was joking and then, as the minutes rolled on, felt hurt and slightly wobbly. But when she'd looked over and seen him standing there anxiously scanning the crowds, his six-foot-three frame inches above everyone else's, she'd known just as surely as she'd ever known anything before in her life. They were meant to be together.

Back at James's flat, it was as if they'd never been apart. And though they'd only had lunch together twice in the last twenty years, they were instantly as close as it was possible to be. Later on, gazing into each other's eyes, Jane asked seriously: 'How do you think this is going to go?'

James remembered everything Dominic had said about not getting involved and taking a step back and playing it cool, not giving anything away. And then, just as quickly as he remembered it, he blanked it from his mind.

'I think I'm going to fall in love with you,' he said.

The day after Jane's arrival, they booked into a hotel in the centre of Edinburgh under the name Mr and Mrs Beresford-Wylie. It was the kind of 24 hours that usually only exists in Meg Ryan romantic comedies. Walking around Edinburgh, Jane wrapped up in James's coat, a man came up to talk to them. 'I can tell you're married,' he said unprompted.

Everything was so perfect. Getting ready to go out to dinner, Jane put on a knock-'em-dead black dress with heels. Opening the door to go ahead to the lift, she noticed a couple coming along the corridor and couldn't resist.

'Same time next week, then,' she called to a bemused James. 'If you want me again, just ask for Tallulah!'

'Will do. And thanks for everything,' shouted James, catching on quickly.

Seeing the horrified look on the couple's faces as they

went down in the lift, James and Jane could hardly keep a straight face, and as soon as they were alone they collapsed into giggles. After such a disastrous relationship history it was amazing for each of them to be with someone who was so in tune, who so completely 'got' them.

Wednesday came all too quickly. Jane cried all the way to the airport and James too was battling to keep the tears at bay. At the security gate, they hugged each other wordlessly, neither wanting to say the word 'goodbye'. Jane was going to see her mum and then to her dad's in Bristol from Friday night, until it was time for her flight back to Australia on Sunday. James would be staying on in Edinburgh until his usual trip back 'home' at the weekend. After their magical few days, it seemed they were destined to go back to being the cyber pen-pals they always had been.

'Maybe we could meet up in Bristol at the weekend, just for half an hour or so,' Jane suggested, her eyes red with crying.

But James just shook his head miserably. He was going back to see his girlfriend. How would he explain why he had to rush out? And besides, another half an hour with Jane would just prolong the agony. He didn't think he could face another goodbye like this one.

And then she was gone, disappearing around the corner, her dark head bent in misery.

All through the rest of that seemingly endless week, James tried to blank what was happening out of his mind. Instead, he went over and over the moments he'd had with Jane, reliving each kiss, each in-depth late-night conversation. It wasn't real life, he told himself. It was just a fantastic dream that he'd be able to tuck away in a little memory box and take out every now and then when things got rough.

On that Friday, he flew down to Bristol with a heavy heart, unsure how he could face his girlfriend again after all that had happened, hoping that she wouldn't be able to read the evidence of his betrayal writ large over his face. But even as he made his way from the airport, he knew he'd been wrong – he had to see Jane again. After being on the other side of the world for each other for so long, it suddenly seemed unthinkable for them to be in the same place, and not to see each other. He called Jane's father, Paul, whom he'd never met. 'I realise you don't know me, but I wonder if I could pop round to your house later after Jane arrives,' he asked, nervously.

Paul, who'd been looking forward to spending some one-on-one time with his Australia-based daughter, was understandably none too thrilled, but reluctantly agreed James could come round – and, yes OK, he'd keep it a secret.

Later that evening, James made an excuse to his girlfriend and, heart thudding in his ears like a drum 'n' bass track, set off to find Jane's dad's house. His nervous knock was answered by Paul, who stood for one full minute, sizing him up, before going off into the kitchen to find Jane.

James could hear Jane's shriek from the hallway as she realised who was at the door and then suddenly there she was, throwing herself into his arms. They embraced like two people who hadn't seen each other for years, rather than a couple who'd said goodbye just a couple of days before.

Instantly, they both knew there could be no going back to their 'other lives' after this. Their relationship was too intense, too 'right' to be put away in a box marked 'special memories'. They had to be together. Now all they had to do was work out how.

✳   ✳   ✳

That night, James went back to his girlfriend knowing he had to end things, but completely unable to think of how. A couple of days with Jane had brought home to him just how unhealthy his relationship was, and how desperately he needed to get out of it. Acting on autopilot, he went through the motions of a normal Friday night, getting a takeaway, watching the telly. But something must have given him away.

The next morning, his girlfriend turned to him with a strange look on her face.

'You don't love me any more, do you?'

It was the opening James needed.

'No,' he admitted miserably. And that was that.

A short time later, he jumped in the car to go to the post office and rang Jane, who was out shopping.

'I need to know if you're definitely moving back from Australia,' he asked her.

'Yes,' she answered, immediately concerned by the urgency in his voice. 'Why?'

'Because I've just ended my relationship.'

There was no going back.

James spent that evening with Jane and her father and step-mum, talking about what they were going to do, making plans for the future. Then, on Sunday, he drove her to Heathrow airport. On the car stereo was a CD he'd made her in Edinburgh, when he thought he'd never see her again, full of tracks that reflected his feelings for her. Listening to songs like 'How Deep is Your Love', 'Better Together' and 'No One Said it Would Be Easy', both struggled to speak, gazing out at the passing countryside with blurry, unseeing eyes. Once again they were both tearful about their approaching separation, but this time the tears were mixed with hope.

Still, Jane was inconsolable when it came time to walk away. James could see her shoulders shaking with sobs even as she went through into departures and out of sight. Before he'd even left the car park, she was on the phone. 'I've just spoken to my boyfriend in Australia,' she told him. 'He knows something's up.'

All through the long drive back and the next couple of interminable days, James thought of Jane and agonised about what kind of reception she'd had back at home. Had she taken one look at her boyfriend and decided she wanted to stay with him after all? Had he persuaded her to give him one more chance?

By the time he finally got to speak to her on Tuesday, he was a nervous wreck. But he needn't have worried. 'I've ended it with my boyfriend, moved out of the house and given my notice in,' she told him triumphantly. She just had to work out her month's notice, and then she was free to come back. That's when their life could begin.

It was the longest five weeks of James's life. Although he spoke to Jane every day – running up a whopping £2,200 bill on his mobile phone – he couldn't stop worrying about her changing her mind and backing out. Even after she'd booked her flight home, for 17 December 2006, he couldn't get rid of the nagging doubts in his mind.

When she rang him at 4.30am, her time, he was convinced it could only mean one thing: bad news.

'Don't be daft,' she giggled. 'I just rang to tell you I'm going out on a run.'

'At half-past four in the morning?'

'I want to look my best when I come into that arrivals lounge.'

But a couple of hours later she wasn't sounding so bubbly.

'I've done something to my foot while I was running,' she groaned. 'It's really painful and swollen.'

Jane had broken her ankle.

'The doctors say I can't fly back before Christmas,' she told James miserably.

It was a devastating blow. James was more convinced than ever that the extra time in Australia would persuade Jane that she was crazy to be thinking of chucking it all in for a guy she'd hardly seen since schooldays. A few weeks more over there and he might never see her again.

But Jane, equally disappointed, wasn't about to give up without a struggle. She got her GP to refer her to a specialist, who gave her the first glimmer of hope. If she flew business class and had blood-thinning injections prior to leaving, she could come home.

James was euphoric, but he knew he wouldn't be able to completely relax until she was back safely in his arms. As the day of her departure dawned, his body felt like a tangle of nerves, each one uncomfortably, painfully alive. His agitation only increased when he rang Jane while she was in the departures lounge to discover that she was with her ex-boyfriend, who'd turned up to say goodbye.

After that, there was silence. Jane didn't ring from the stop-off in Dubai, despite James sending dozens of ever-more-frantic texts, and he became increasingly convinced that she had changed her mind. She hadn't got on the plane after all. She'd gone back to patch things up with her ex.

With a heavy feeling of foreboding, he set off for the airport on 17 December, secretly convinced it was a wasted trip. She wouldn't come. He was sure of it.

Her plane landed and passengers from her flight started to file through into the arrivals lounge. James scanned their faces, scarcely allowing himself to blink for fear of missing her. One after another they came, at first in dribs and drabs, then a whole surge of passengers together, and then finally the last remaining stragglers. Jane was nowhere to be seen.

She hadn't come. He'd been right all along.

And then the swing doors opened and a little, limping figure appeared, slowly making her way forward, leaning heavily on crutches.

Jane.

Without stopping to think, James ran forward and picked her up, swinging her round, oblivious either to the amused faces of the onlookers or to the crutches falling to the ground.

She was here.

Afterwards, he learned how she'd been frantic when her Aussie mobile phone refused to work in Dubai and, stranded in her wheelchair, she hadn't been able to find anyone to wheel her to a phone. For hours she'd sat there miserably, knowing he'd be going out of his mind with worry, but unable to get a message to him.

❅   ❅   ❅

After nearly two decades in which their relationship had pretty much hung in suspended animation, suddenly things started happening very quickly once Jane arrived back in the UK.

On 22 December, James dropped theatrically to one knee in front of Jane's wheelchair outside a jeweller's shop in Edinburgh, oblivious to the rain-sodden surface of the pavement, and asked her to marry him.

Then, on 24 February 2007, the day after Jane's 38th birthday, they tied the knot at a romantic manor house hotel in Castle Combe.

Now based in Ledbury, Herefordshire, the couple are doing their best to make up for all the lost time, and to focus on the next forty years, rather than the last twenty. Sometimes they reminisce about the reunion that broke their silence, but which very nearly broke James's heart. And other times they think way back to when they were school kids, and starting a relationship was as easy as scribbling a note on a piece of scrap paper.

And the new Mrs Beresford-Wylie always smiles when she remembers turning to a 13-year-old James and saying: 'I should marry you, you know. I like your name much better than mine.'

Out of the mouths of babes...

CHAPTER FOUR
WHAT GOES AROUND...

William felt the sweat trickle down under his arms as he made his way through the deserted school corridors, eerily silent without the usual cacophony of children's voices and doors slamming, to the little-used side entrance. The playground stretched ahead, empty and exposed, the net-less goalposts at each end seeming suddenly so much larger without a scrum of bodies clustered around them or the usual grey school-regulation jumpers fluttering from the top bar, where they'd been casually looped over.

Crossing the seemingly vast expanse of grey tarmac, his shoulders bowed under the weight of his groaning school bag, William's eyes constantly flitted from side to side, looking for any sign of movement. A couple of times, he'd think he saw something and his whole body would freeze, only to realise it had been the wind blowing through the branches of a tree or a bird suddenly appearing in his peripheral vision.

Surely he'd left it long enough. They wouldn't have hung around all this time, would they? They'd have got bored of waiting and moved off in search of some other distraction, some other victim.

The gates were growing closer now, looming up ahead with their institutional black bars festooned with heavy chains, as yet unfastened. William knew that once he was through those gates, it was just a case of putting one foot in front of the other and running as fast as he could for the three-quarters of a mile back to his home, and hoping against hope not to hear the sickening thud of footsteps following behind.

He was out of luck.

As soon as he'd stepped through the gates, he saw them, leaning back against the school wall, ties shoved into pockets, from where they trailed down like jauntily striped bunting against the dark-grey uniform trousers. There were four of them today. That meant it was going to be a bad one.

'Oi, Rice. You're late. We've been waiting for you.' It was Carl Allen, the ringleader, a thin smirk breaking up his pink, spotty face. 'Anyone would think you were trying to avoid us.'

William swallowed hard, trying to think.

'I, er, had to stay late,' he said, hating the way his nervousness made his voice sound weak and squeaky. 'Anyway, I'd better go. I'm late.'

He took off quickly in the opposite direction from where they were standing, knowing that whichever way he went they'd follow him. Sure enough, he heard their unhurried footsteps behind him.

Please don't let them hurt me, he found himself praying internally, although he was never quite sure who it was he was hoping could help him. *Please don't let them hurt me.*

But his prayers went unheeded as a foot came out and caught him as he ran, sending him flying through the air, his bag coming free from his shoulder and landing somewhere behind where he landed, sprawling face down.

'Oh, I'm sorry, did I trip you up?' James Long was leaning over him, his ferrety features arranged into an expression of mock concern that would have carried more conviction if he hadn't been going through William's pockets at the same time looking for any coins he might have had left over from his lunch money.

Meanwhile, the other three were emptying out his bag, shaking open each book in case he had any money hidden inside the pages.

'Don't suppose you'll be needing all this scrap paper, will you?' said Carl Allen, holding up the geography project William had been working on for the last two weeks. William winced as he watched the pages he'd spent so much time on being crumpled up and tossed carelessly into the road like unwanted rubbish.

Satisfied they'd got all they could from his bag, his four tormentors started to move off, but just as William tried to haul himself painfully to his feet, he felt another kick land in his back, sending him sprawling back down again.

Hearing their snorts of laughter as they moved off down the road, William felt his face burning and tears of pain and humiliation sprung to his eyes. Getting unsteadily to his feet, he looked down and saw that the knee of his trousers was torn. Again. His mum would be furious, but he didn't dare tell her the truth in case she made a stink up at the school like last time, which had just made everything so much worse.

Picking up his books, which lay strewn over the pavement, William could hardly see through the veil of water that blurred his eyes. *One day I'll show them*, he vowed to himself trying to smooth down the sheets of crumpled paper he'd rescued from the road. *One day they'll be sorry.*

It was spring 1981 and William was 12 years old. He had no clue, as he blinked back hot tears of shame, that it would be 24 long years before he got his wish.

❋   ❋   ❋

The news came, as news in the Rice family often did, from William's older sister Kate. 'There's a 20-year reunion for your year at school,' she told him over the phone. 'It's not for another month, so there's no excuse for not going. All the details are on that reuniting website.'

William gave a snort of derision. 'Seeing as I couldn't get out of that dump fast enough, I'm hardly likely to rush back there voluntarily, am I?' he pointed out reasonably.

Kate wasn't deterred. 'Come on, Will,' she said. 'You had some good mates in that school. And anyway, aren't you tempted to go back there and show them all just how well you've done?'

William put the phone down and gazed pensively around his spacious office, located on the corner of a converted factory in an achingly trendy part of the East End, with floor-to-ceiling windows that afforded him an impressive view over the rooftops of the neighbouring flats and offices. The furniture was modern and expensive-looking – in addition to his large state-of-the art desk, there was also a 'relaxing area' with a soft black leather sofa and chairs. As lawyer to one of the leading broker's firms, William really had, as Kate said, showed them.

He had the six-figure salary and the lifestyle to go with it. A large flat overlooking a garden square in Fulham that he shared with his fiancée, Alexandra, plus a cottage in Devon and a villa in Italy, which he'd bought on impulse while holidaying around Lake Como two years before.

At 36, he had everything he'd ever dreamed of. Funny though, how just the mention of his schooldays back in Watford had stirred up all the long-buried insecurities. It was indeed twenty years since his year group had reached 16 and divided up – some, like him, going on to sixth form. Others, like Allen and Long, disappearing back into whatever subdivision of society they belonged, no doubt finding new victims whose lives they could enjoy ruining.

He hadn't thought about them in years, so it was strange now how vividly the memories came back to him. He remembered how the problems had started just a few weeks into his first term at the new secondary school he'd had to join when his parents moved house. He'd been small for his age then and, not having had time to form a group of friends, easy prey for the bullies.

It had begun with them asking to 'borrow' money, but had rapidly graduated to regular extortion and physical abuse. How clearly he remembered hanging round at school long after the final bell had gone, hoping his tormentors would have got bored and gone home, and the shame of having his mother or older sisters try to intervene on his behalf, knowing it would only make things worse for him in the long run.

As he'd moved up through the school, gathering a

group of close friends around him and shooting up suddenly at 14 to his adult height of six foot, William had outgrown the bullies, and they'd gradually moved on to younger, easier targets. He thought he'd put those early humiliating days far behind him, but Kate's phone call brought it all rushing back. Looking back, he could see that those memories had probably always been there, just under the surface, spurring him on to do better and achieve more – to make sure that, whatever happened, he always came out on top.

Kate had directed him to look at the entry about the reunion on the website. Even though he'd heard a lot about Friends Reunited since it had started up a few years before, he'd always avoided looking on there. He'd kept in touch with the school friends he was closest to and he had no interest in knowing what had happened to the others.

And yet all the rest of that afternoon, the thought niggled away in the back of his mind. He hadn't thought of any of those people in years, and yet now he couldn't get them out of his head. Would it hurt to look?

After signing up for membership, he started looking through the pages of names of people he'd gone to school with, occasionally stopping at a name he remembered and double-clicking to see their profiles. Inwardly he chuckled when he saw some of the more fanciful entries. How many 'successful businessmen' could his class of losers really have produced? How could so many people claim to be 'happily married' to the love of their lives, and all with such 'gorgeous, perfect' children?

But when he got to Carl Allen's entry, he stopped laughing. Just the sight of his former tormentor's name was enough to make William's skin grow clammy and his mouth dry. He double-clicked on his entry and discovered that Allen was now putting himself forward as a family man with – surprise, surprise – a successful carpentry business. 'Life's been good to me,' he bragged in his profile.

William felt sick. Until that moment he hadn't realised how much he was hoping to discover that Allen's life had been a hard one, full of failure and disappointment. Or at least that he'd suffered some kind of remorse for the things he'd done to people at school. There wasn't anything in the brief, chirpy profile that gave William any sense of satisfaction or closure. Instead, he found himself seething at the unfairness of it all. Why had Allen's life turned out so well when he'd thought nothing of trying to ruin so many other people's? Where was the justice in him growing up into a happy adult without even acknowledging the misery he'd inflicted as a child?

James Long's entry was shorter, but provided little more in the way of satisfaction. He was divorced, but in a 'fantastic new relationship' and working a desk job in a sales department. As far as William could see there'd been no comeuppance for his nasty behaviour, no prison sentences, no great tragedy. Nothing. In fact, both bullies seemed to have got off scot-free.

Which is why William decided he would go to the reunion after all. If nothing else he could, as Kate said, show them all what he'd made of his life. Despite their claims of success, William couldn't imagine many of his former classmates enjoyed quite the lifestyle he did, or the bank balance. At least he'd have the satisfaction of proving to them that they hadn't defeated him.

Over the next few weeks, William contacted Jack and Lucy, the two school friends he'd remained in contact with, and begged, threatened and finally bribed them to come back to the reunion with him.

'It had better be good,' said Lucy, referring not to the event itself but to the slap-up meal William had promised to buy them as payment for accompanying him.

The reunion was to be held in the function room of a hotel in Watford, William's home town. When he confirmed attendance with the organiser and was sent a list of all the other confirmed guests, William was both pleased and horrified to see Allen and Long's names among the others. Although he wanted them to be there, at the same time he was dreading seeing them again.

'You'll be absolutely fine, Will,' Kate told him. He'd travelled to Watford straight from work on the Friday night to give him plenty of time to settle his nerves before the reunion the following evening. Kate and his other sister, Lou, had both come round to their parents' modest semi to give him a pep talk. 'Just make sure you wear that Paul Smith suit – it probably cost more than Allen's house!' William smiled, but inside he felt a faint twinge of nausea that transported him immediately back more than two decades in time to when he was a small-for-his-age young lad, spending his break times hiding in the toilets in case the bullies were waiting for him outside. How was he going to cope tomorrow, if just the mention of their names caused such an extreme reaction?

The following evening, William dressed with extreme care before setting off to meet Jack and Lucy in what used to be one of their favourite pubs, near to the hotel where the reunion was taking place.

'I feel like a complete wreck,' he complained, knocking back the whisky he'd ordered to steady his nerves. Jack and Lucy, who'd both managed to escape the attentions of the bullies while at school, sympathised but told him he had to keep reminding himself who it was who'd got out of Watford and got himself the smart London flat, the gorgeous girlfriend, the flash car.

However, as they made their way the short distance from the pub to the hotel, William found the burst of confidence the whisky and pep talk had given him evaporating into the chill spring air. To his vexation, he felt his palms becoming damp and his breathing shallower.

'Remember, you're to stick to my sides like glue,' he instructed his companions. They nodded wearily, having already reassured him of this several times over the last couple of hours.

Climbing the steps to the hotel lobby, William had a sudden urge to turn around and bolt back to the pub, or back to his parents' house or, best of all, back to London where he belonged. But, taking a deep breath, he allowed himself to be ushered through the carpeted lobby and down a corridor into the function room.

As their eyes slowly adjusted to the dim lighting, the three friends could make out various groups of people standing dotted around the room. Most, from what they could see, were already in fairly advanced stages of inebriation.

They hadn't been standing there long when a yelp went up from one of the neighbouring knots of people.

'Oh my God, it's Jack and Will!'

They found themselves manhandled over into a corner, where they were confronted by several smiling faces they vaguely remembered and a couple they couldn't recall at all.

It quickly became apparent that while time had been kind to some, it had enjoyed a veritable field day with others. A couple of the girls on whom William had cherished secret teenaged crushes had expanded so alarmingly as to be almost unrecognisable, while the erstwhile school heartthrob was now sporting hair that was as thin as his beer belly clearly was not.

And then he saw them.

Across the room, leaning against the bar trying to give the impression of being completely at ease by talking over-loudly, while all the time darting nervous looks around the room, were Carl Allen and James Long – although, to be frank, William wouldn't have recognised Allen if he hadn't been standing next to his one-time best mate.

To say Allen had aged badly would be an understatement – he had aged *atrociously*. The spots of his youth had been replaced by a florid, pink complexion that spoke of rather too many pints and too few fresh vegetables. His face had a raw, meaty look to it and his small, mean eyes were all but hidden by fleshy pouches of skin. The heavy gold jewellery he was wearing did little to disguise the fact that Allen's shiny, ill-fitting suit appeared to have been made for a much slimmer man.

Long looked pretty much the same – his thin, weaselly features maybe slightly less sharp than they used to be, but the same unmistakable sneer.

They were standing with two women who were obviously their partners and whose hard, care-worn faces already showed unmistakable signs of how they'd look in middle age.

'Look over there,' hissed Lucy, unnecessarily. But William was already standing rigid, feeling that old petrified impotency wash over him as if the last twenty years had never happened and he was once again that scared, humiliated boy.

'Let's go talk to them,' Jack suggested.

William shook his head, turning back to the others in their group.

'Some people never change, do they?' said one of the women, indicating the two at the bar with a jerk of her head. 'They were both tossers twenty years ago, and they're tossers now.'

It should have made William feel better, but it didn't. The truth was he *knew* Allen and Long weren't worth losing sleep over. He could see just by looking at them that their jumped-up claims to success on the website had been fabrications of their own self-inflated imaginations. And yet he was furious with himself for letting them make him feel like this. These two ignorant, rather pitiful men still had power over him, even after all this time, and it made him feel frustrated, angry and irrationally terrified all at the same time. Just what was the matter with him?

'Just ignore them,' Lucy told him. 'You've done what you came to do, Will. Everyone's talking about how great you look, and how they all knew you'd be one of the big success stories.' (Yeah, right!) 'What do you care what those two losers think?'

But, much to his own annoyance, William did care, and he knew that if he didn't go and confront his old tormentors, there'd be a part of him that would always know he'd let them win. 'I'm going over there,' he told his friends.

Ignoring their restraining hands on his arm, William crossed the floor of the room, vaguely aware of Jack and Lucy hurrying after him.

Standing behind Allen, William hesitated a moment before tapping him on the shoulder. 'Remember me?' he asked, his face stretched painfully into a forced smile.

A confused look came into Allen's eyes as he attempted to place him before giving up, with a half smile. 'You look familiar, mate, but I'm terrible with names.'

'It's William Rice.' By a tremendous force of will, William managed to keep his voice level. 'You and your sidekick here used to make my life hell.'

Allen clearly thought this was some kind of joke. 'Did we? Yeah, well, kids can get a bit rough sometimes can't they? Still, no hard feelings hey, mate?' With that, he held one of his square, meaty hands out in a gesture of reconciliation, revealing a chunky gold bracelet around his wrist.

'You weren't just a bit rough,' William went on in the same clear, calm tone. 'You – and that one,' he nodded towards Long, 'were a couple of cowardly bullies who picked on anyone smaller than yourselves. And I think it's time for you to apologise.'

Even right up until the words were out of his mouth, William hadn't known what he was about to say. But now it was said, he realised it was true. He needed an apology from these two, some kind of acknowledgement of what they'd put him through.

By this time a small crowd had gathered around to listen to what was going on and, across the sudden embarrassed hush that descended, he could hear someone whispering: 'Dead right.'

Allen had lowered his hand and was gazing back at William, blinking rapidly as if not quite sure if this was some elaborate wind-up. Long, meanwhile, was smirking as usual, but from the way he was gripping his glass, it was clear he was not enjoying being the centre of all this not-entirely-friendly scrutiny.

'Don't be stupid. All that was years ago. Live and let live, hey?'

Allen made a show of turning his back on William. But one of the onlookers who'd been watching the whole scenario unfold stepped in front of him. William vaguely recognised him as Danny, another of the 'misfits' from the year group.

'Actually, while you're at it, I wouldn't mind an apology either,' he said. 'You made my life completely miserable.'

'And mine,' someone else piped up.

William wouldn't have thought it was possible for the already florid Allen to blush, but his face turned unmistakably darker at finding himself the centre of all this unwanted attention. 'Look. I'm just here to enjoy myself, right?' he appealed to the knot of people around him. 'We don't want no trouble.'

'Funny, we didn't want any trouble either, all those years ago,' William told him. 'But I don't recall that cutting much ice with you.'

Long was now looking decidedly uncomfortable and the two women with them were whispering furiously to each other.

'Just apologise, and we can all move on with our evening,' said Danny, levelly.

Seeing that they were actually serious, the mood of the two former bullies turned from jocular blokiness to defensiveness. 'I can't believe this,' muttered James Long. 'I only came for a few drinks and a bit of a laugh and now we're getting all this aggro from twenty years ago.'

'It's not aggro,' said William pleasantly, still not entirely sure where this sudden cool bravado was coming from. 'It's just a polite request for you to say sorry to all the people you upset when we were at school.'

Now Long and Allen were visibly uncomfortable: Allen was sweating profusely and William could see where a vein in Long's temple was throbbing painfully. He had a sudden realisation. Now he was the one doing the bullying – and it was the turn of the other two to feel that mixture of rage and humiliation that comes from knowing you're outnumbered and that you're powerless to stand up for yourself.

'This is fucking ridiculous,' Allen spat eventually, his face the colour of the wine his wife was downing at breakneck speed. 'I never could stand any of you lot when we was at school, and you're all still a bunch of fucking losers. I'm off.'

And with that, he grabbed his wife's arm roughly and pushed angrily through the knot of onlookers, throwing William a look as he did so that William recognised only too well. It was the look he himself had worn so many times as a boy – a look of fear and loathing, mixed together with sheer 'why is this happening?' confusion. And then, with a furious-looking James Long following close behind, they were gone.

The whole encounter couldn't have taken more than five minutes, and most of the guests were still chatting on quite unaware any drama had taken place, but to William it was as though time had stood still. In those few minutes, all the baggage he'd been lugging around without even knowing for the last twenty-odd years was laid out before him, and then made to magically disappear. He felt suddenly lighter, different – as though he was no longer exactly the same person who'd walked into the hotel not even an hour before.

Jack and Lucy were beside themselves with glee. 'What a result, hey?' Jack whooped. 'Did you *see* the look on Allen's face?'

As William and Danny exchanged glances, though, the expression in their eyes wasn't one of triumph but of finality. That night, something had been completed that had been left unfinished for too long. And now it was time to move on.

Leaving the hotel later that night, Lucy was convinced Allen and Long would be waiting outside – with a whole bunch of their mates. 'Don't worry. They won't be there,' William told her with certainty.

He didn't really know why he was so sure, but there was something about the way the two of them had slunk out of the venue, looking so much smaller than when they'd stood at the bar just a few moments before, that told him beyond any doubt that he wouldn't be seeing either of them again.

❋   ❋   ❋

Three years on, and William is now married with an 18-month-old son.

'Sometimes when I look at him, I feel so anxious

about everything that's in store for him,' he admits. 'Children can be so cruel to one another. But if my experience has taught me anything it's that justice will usually be done – even if you have to wait twenty years for it.

'And you know what, revenge is sweet – don't let anyone tell you any different.'

CHAPTER FIVE
'MYSPACE, MY FAMILY'

'You know, I might just try putting her name into MySpace or something.'

Sabrina Bailey looked away from the movie they were watching, and studied her 26-year-old husband's face with amusement. She didn't even need to ask who he was talking about. By now she knew all too well.

Ever since she'd met Leon, and in fact way before then, he'd been searching for his birth mother, always coming up with different leads, different theories, but all of them had come to nothing.

A few years back, they'd had a brief flurry of excitement when Leon had heard back from the agency in Suffolk, England, which had dealt with Leon's adoption back in the mid-1980s. In answer to his letter about his birth parents, they'd guardedly revealed they

TAMMY COHEN

did have an index card that might be of interest to him, but he'd have to visit in person before they could release any details.

It had been the most frustrating of experiences. One moment the high of finally getting a concrete link to the woman who'd given birth to him, and the next the crashing disappointment of realising the card that might contain the key to his questions, was still out of reach... because Leon and Sabrina lived in Houston, Texas, thousands of miles away from the adoption agency that had dealt with his birth. A young couple with two small children, it would take them years to save the money for him to travel to the UK on what might yet turn out to be another wild goose chase.

But Leon hadn't given up. He'd started putting money by for the trip, and was constantly thinking of new ways of tracing his birth mother. The MySpace idea, though it came out of the blue, wasn't as extreme as some of the other schemes he'd come up with.

While she carried on watching the movie that sultry evening in July 2008, Leon sat down at the computer, logging onto his MySpace account, as he always did. Scrolling down onto the Find Friends facility, he typed in the name he knew so well he could have spelled it in his sleep. Debra Kneuman.

At least it's not a common name he thought for the millionth time, as he idly waited for the results to come up. In fact, so unusual was it that the chances were he wouldn't find any matches at all.

He was surprised therefore, when two possible matches popped up on the screen. 'Hey,' he yelled across to Sabrina. 'You'll never guess what – TWO Debra Kneumans!'

Sabrina jumped up and joined him at the computer, scrutinising the two thumbnail-sized photos. 'Well, you can rule that one out,' she said, pointing to a picture of a girl obviously too young to be Leon's mother.

That just left one possibility: a woman with hair scraped back into a ponytail, wearing sunglasses and a big smile. When they clicked on the profile page, they found she was 40 – approximately the age Leon's birth mother would be now. But just as he was starting to get excited, his hopes were dashed again. He knew his birth mother was British, as was his father. The woman on the profile page was listed as living in New Hampshire, USA.

'You've got to write to her anyway,' Sabrina told him. 'It's such an unusual name, there's got to be a chance it's her.'

But when he started to scroll down the page, Leon had another disappointment. Debra Kneuman had last logged onto her MySpace page eight months before. It could be another eight months or even years before she checked in again.

'Go have a look at her friends list,' Sabrina suggested. 'Maybe you could get a message to her through them.' Debra Kneuman had only one 'friend' on her contacts list – a young woman called Natalie. 'Leave a message for her too,' was Sabrina's advice.

Leon chose his words carefully. 'I'm trying to get in touch with Debra Kneuman,' he wrote. 'If you're in contact with her can you please ask her to check her MySpace page?'

Then came the worst part. The waiting. Leon was torn between not wanting to get his hopes up, and being swept up in insuppressible excitement. 'It *can't* be her,' he'd say one minute, remembering the New Hampshire tag line. The next minute, he'd be talking about jumping on a plane and tracking down the New Hampshire town on the woman's web page and knocking on every door until he found her.

Every morning, the first thing Leon did was check his MySpace inbox, hoping against hope to see her name appear. All through the day, he'd check in at intervals, each time his heart going into overdrive as he waited for the page to refresh, then nose-diving once he realised she hadn't been in touch. Then finally, three weeks after his initial approach, he had a message. It was from Natalie, the 'friend' they'd asked for help. 'Yes, I know Debra Kneuman,' she wrote. 'She's my mom. How come you're trying to get in touch with her?'

Leon stared at the screen open mouthed before shrieking: 'Sabrina! Sabrina! I just got a message from a woman who could be my *sister*!'

Sabrina knew just what this meant to Leon. He'd grown up with just one other sibling – an adopted sister. Although his adopted family had always been good to him, he'd felt right from the beginning that he wanted to know the people who'd made him, particularly the woman who'd given birth to him. He'd actually been looked after by her until he was two years old, so he knew there had been a relationship there at one time that he'd somehow been missing all his life.

He'd been told when he was very young that he was adopted. As soon as he was old enough to understand, his adoptive parents had given him a letter his birth mother had asked them to pass on. In it, she talked about how hard it had been to make the decision to give him up, and how she hoped he'd now have a better life than she'd have been able to give him. She was just 14 when she'd had him, she told him. She just wasn't ready to look after a child properly.

Leon had always known his natural parents were British. His adoptive parents were Americans, but as they were in the military they'd moved around a lot – England, Louisiana, finally ending up in Texas, where he still lived.

When he was 18, he'd found some letters relating to

his adoption that had given him his natural mother's full name and also led him to the agency that had arranged the adoption all those years before. But then had come the disappointing news that he'd have to wait until he raised enough money for a ticket to England just to find out if the agency had any more details to give him.

All these years he'd wanted to find out news of who he was and where he came from, and now here he was looking at a picture of someone who might well turn out to be the sister he never knew he had.

'Send her a message. Quickly!' Sabrina was almost more excited than Leon. But they both knew they had to be careful. If Debra *was* his mother and she hadn't told her daughter anything about him, revealing who he thought he was might open up a monumental can of worms.

'Can you please ask your mom if she knows anyone by the name of Leon Bailey?' he wrote eventually, adding his number as an afterthought, his fingers trembling as he tapped the keyboard.

Then, just like before, there was nothing else to do but wait.

＊　　＊　　＊

Debra Kneuman screamed so loudly down the phone, her daughter thought something was seriously wrong. This Leon Bailey guy must be pretty important to have provoked this kind of reaction. 'Oh my God!' Debra gasped, when she could finally bring herself to speak. 'I don't know about the surname, but the only person I know called Leon is my oldest son!'

Now it was Natalie's turn to shriek. Ever since she was a kid she and her two sisters and younger brother had been told about the baby their mom had had to give up for adoption. Their whole lives had been lived in the shadow of the older brother they'd never met. On his birthday, 12 February, they'd all remember him and wish him happy birthday, and hope that wherever he was, he was celebrating with people who loved him. They'd all dreamed at various points, of finding him, and getting to know him. And now she found out she'd already been in touch with him, without having a clue who he was!

As soon as she put the phone down, she went straight back to the computer to message the mystery correspondent. '*I'm your sister!!!!!!*' she told him, still scarcely able to believe it herself. Then she added her mum's number, and told him Debra was waiting for him to call.

When Leon had dreamed about this moment in the past – the moment he finally had his birth mother's number in his hands – he'd imagined himself feverishly dialling the numbers, desperate to hear her voice. But now it was actually here, he couldn't bring himself to act. Instead, he sat quietly for a few moments, just getting hold of himself.

Like most people, Leon had seen his share of movies and TV reality shows where adopted children finally trace their birth mothers only to be rejected or find they've died, or become senile. What if he rang her and she didn't want to know? What if he was a skeleton she never wanted to release from the closet?

He was still trying to build up his courage when the phone rang.

'Leon?' the tone was uncertain, but throbbing with barely suppressed excitement. 'It's your mom.'

All Leon's concerns melted away in the warmth of this stranger's voice. And within seconds it was as if she wasn't a stranger at all. Over the next thirty or forty minutes, Debra and Leon caught up on each other's lives. Debra told him all about his brother and sisters and how they'd been wanting to meet him. She told him about how she'd looked after him until he was two, and what he was like as a little boy and how she'd dreamed for the last 25 years of finding him again.

One of the first things she asked him was the question that had been burning into her head and her heart ever since she'd signed away her rights to her son and handed him over to strangers.

'Have you had a good life?' She needed to hear that he'd been cared for and loved, that her sacrifice hadn't been for nothing. She was almost weak with relief when Leon told her that though he and his adoptive parents had had their share of ups and downs, like any family, he had no complaints.

'I didn't know any better,' Debra told him, trying to explain how young she'd been, and how hard she'd tried. 'I just wanted you to have the best possible chance in life.'

It was the conversation each had imagined a thousand times, and after it was over it felt as something had been completed in their lives that before had felt incomplete, as if someone had taken a pencil and shaded in the blank areas of a drawing.

When Debra put the phone down on her first-born son, her head was still buzzing. After all this time, all these years, all the tears, he'd found her *via a website!* She still couldn't quite comprehend it. Talking to Leon had been like opening up a floodgate through which a torrent of memories now poured out. She remembered how naïve she'd been at 13 when she first got pregnant, how little she'd understood of what it meant to be a mother.

She'd been living with foster parents at the time after a turbulent relationship with her real parents. She remembered how fiercely she'd loved her baby, and yet how difficult she'd found being a parent when still only a child herself. She'd been so ill equipped to look after someone else. No one had ever shown her how to do it properly.

She remembered too, Tony Goulbourne, Leon's dad. Tall, handsome and himself still barely old enough to buy a pint in a pub, let alone become a father. She'd been so bowled over by him, and carried away by how well they got on, not realising that having a laugh together was a very long way from having a child together. They'd stopped seeing each other by the time she realised she was pregnant and, though he'd tried to hide it, she knew he hadn't been that keen on the idea of becoming a dad.

After Leon was born, Tony had seen his baby a few times and, together with his mum, had formed quite an attachment to the little boy, but when she'd moved down to London with her new boyfriend, they'd completely lost touch. So when – after a few months of struggling with the competing demands of a toddler and a resentful new man – she'd finally realised she couldn't cope, she hadn't even informed Tony that she was putting Leon up for adoption. She'd just assumed he wouldn't be interested.

She'd made that agonising decision all alone, writing that heartbreaking letter and handing over her baby with no one there to share in her grief. After he'd gone, she'd buried her nose in the little vests and shorts that were left behind, trying to inhale the smell of her little boy to make up for the aching loss of him. The only way she could get through it was to keep telling herself that her baby deserved more than she was able to give him, but no matter how many times she reminded herself of that, it was still a heartbreaking, cataclysmic experience, and one that had dogged her ever since.

For all these years she'd shouldered that responsibility alone, and wept in private over the son she'd given away. Twenty-four years of regretting and wishing and hoping – all done on her own.

But now that miracle she'd been dreaming of had finally happened, she suddenly felt the most over-powering need to find Tony and tell him what had happened. She'd always felt a niggling guilt that she hadn't consulted him about the adoption. When she'd bumped into him in Ipswich a year or so after it had happened and told him about it, she'd been surprised by the flicker of pain that had passed over his face. But she'd never heard anything more from him, so she assumed he'd come to terms with it.

Now, though, she wanted to find him again and let him know their son was safe. She'd no idea whether he'd even thought about her or Leon in all these years, but he deserved to know what had happened to their boy. The only trouble was, she didn't have a clue how to get hold of him after all these years. He could be anywhere.

Then she was struck by a sudden wild idea. If Leon had found her via MySpace, wasn't there just a chance, a faint chance, that she could find Tony the same way.

She switched on her computer…

✳ ✳ ✳

In Ipswich, UK, Tony Goulbourne couldn't understand why his cousins kept ringing him. 'I'm telling you, you've got to look at your MySpace page. There's someone who's really desperate to talk to you.'

At 44, Tony didn't really count himself one of the computer generation. His kids had helped him set up a MySpace account, but he hardly ever looked at it. He just didn't really get the whole Internet thing, and was much more likely to switch on the telly or turn on the music to unwind after a day's work as a senior practitioner, looking after the mentally ill, than start surfing the Net. But his cousin was so insistent, Tony knew there had to be something worth turning on the computer for.

Incredibly, he still remembered his log-in password. Calling up his profile page, he scrolled to the bottom right, where friends can leave messages. He didn't know exactly what he was looking for, but as soon as he saw the picture, he froze. Even after all these years, he still recognised her instantly. Same smile, same eyes. Debbie.

And the second he recognised her, something else also came into his mind. If she was contacting him after all these years, she must have news of their son.

With mounting excitement, he read her message. He was right. Leon had been in touch with her, Debbie told him. He wanted to see Tony. He'd been searching for both of them for years.

As Tony read, a smile came over his face that wouldn't leave him for the rest of the night.

Leon. His boy.

The truth is that, as Tony had grown older, he'd come to regret more and more the lack of responsibility he'd shown when Leon was born. In fact, he now viewed that as the biggest mistake of his life. The births of each of his other children – six boys and a girl – had just reminded him of the other son he'd allowed to slip out of his life. He'd told all of them about their eldest brother, and they'd all shared in the folklore that built up around their missing sibling. His second son in particular had felt the absence of his brother most strongly. It's hard being the oldest and he'd often talked wistfully about what it would be like to have an older brother to turn to.

Tony had only found out later that his mum would have brought Leon up, if they'd been told about the adoption in time. Tony had never even considered it as a possibility, but once he knew, he kept going back over what had happened, wishing he could go back in time and step in to claim his son.

He'd been to see Debbie's mum, but she didn't even know where Debbie was living, only that she'd emigrated to the States. She certainly had no idea which adoption agency her daughter had used. All Tony knew was that Leon's adoptive parents were an American couple who'd been based in Ipswich for a while.

Over the years, various people offered to help him search for his son, but he didn't even have a surname to go on. When he sought advice from another adoption agency, he was told there was nothing he could do.

Of course, Tony loved all his children, but all the time he felt there was a part of his life missing. 'I don't think I'll ever feel complete until I see my son again,' he'd tell his brothers sadly.

When he set up his MySpace profile page, Tony was careful to include the few precious pictures he had of Leon as a baby alongside the photos of his other children. It was his way of saying that he knew he had another son out there, and he hadn't forgotten him – a tribute to the boy he increasingly felt he'd let down. But now, here was Debbie after all these years, with the news he'd been waiting all this time to hear. Even though he was alone in house, Tony found he couldn't stop grinning.

Debra had left her number and Tony rang straight away. It had been a quarter of a century since he'd seen her and yet he'd have known her voice anywhere. She was so excited her words spilled out like firecrackers. 'I've spoken to him. I've spoken to our son,' she told him. 'He found me on the Internet and he wants to find you too.'

Tony understood her excitement when he learned that it was only a few hours earlier that she and Leon had first spoken. No wonder she could hardly get her words out! And he had some news for her too. Debra had lost touch with her parents when she'd gone to the States 15 years before. They'd always had a fraught relationship and she'd convinced herself that they'd be happier not hearing from her. But Tony told her otherwise. 'I went to see them when I was looking for Leon,' he told her. 'They really want to find you, Debbie. They're desperate to see you again.'

So it was that after talking to Tony, Debra made the decision to give her parents another try. Dialling the old number, her mouth went dry as she heard it ringing, her nerve almost failing her, before someone picked it up.

'Mum?' she ventured.

In the space of one evening, Debra had found her son, her ex-boyfriend and her estranged parents. It was as though Leon had opened up a hole in the fence through which all the others were now following.

It was one of the best nights of Debra's life.

As soon as Tony had put the phone down to Debra, he sent a message to Leon using the link she'd given him, not even pausing to consider how best to word it in his haste to get in touch. Then he spent ages scouring the photos on Leon's profile page. It was so impossible to equate this man, this father of two, with the little boy he'd held all those years before. And, as for the news that he was now a grandfather, Tony just didn't know how to take that. When his younger brother had become a granddad, he'd ridiculed him mercilessly. Now it turned out he was one as well – twice over!

As he was still looking at the photos of his long-lost son, a message came up from Leon. Debra must have let him know they'd spoken. Tony replied immediately, and within the space of half an hour they'd sent several messages back and forth, exchanging information about their lives. In one of them, Leon left a telephone number.

Tony stared at it a long time, and then he dialled it.

'Hullo?'

It should have occurred to Tony that his son, his boy, would now have a man's deep voice, but for some reason it still came as an almighty shock.

'Leon?' he ventured.

Leon didn't seem to have any reciprocal doubts about whom he was speaking to. Tony could sense the excitement in his son's voice. But even though he himself was elated, he told himself to keep calm, and he could feel himself holding back a little.

The voice was such a reality check – a reminder of how many years had gone past, how much of each other's history they'd missed out on. This is my son, Tony kept reminding himself. This man, speaking with this man's voice is that same little boy in the photos. It just didn't seem credible.

Leon was so easy to talk to, his enthusiasm carrying the conversation along without any effort, but Tony still found there was something keeping him from being as ebullient as he'd always thought he would be. 'I'm not great at talking on the phone,' he told his son. 'The real talking will come when we finally get together.'

Coming off the phone, he realised that, although he was desperately excited, the thing that was holding him back was fear. He'd wanted this for so long – for all his adult life he'd told people that his life would be completed once he'd found his son. It was almost as if now it was all happening, he was frightened he would no longer have anything left to drive him on. After all, if all your dreams have come true by the age of 44, what is there left to live for?

Back in Texas, however, Leon Bailey had no such reservations.

He was absolutely elated. In one magical, never-to-be-repeated night, he'd gone from having one adopted sister, to eleven half-brothers and -sisters. And he'd found the birth parents he'd wondered about all his life. And all via the Internet. It just didn't seem possible.

And yet, it was. He and Sabrina studied the photos on the computer screen for hours. Surely Izaiah had his grandmother's eyes? And didn't little Alexus look a bit like Leon's dad? For the first time in his life, Leon was able to look for family resemblances, and he was relishing every moment of it.

After that momentous night in July 2008, Leon's

whole life changed. Now, in addition to his adoptive family, he also had a whole big, new, extended family, and he lost no time in arranging to meet them.

In September 2008, three months after he'd first idly inputted his birth mother's name into MySpace, Leon and Debra met for the first time. They'd been talking almost non-stop in the interim, long phone calls that went on late into the night, trying to catch up on a lifetime of experiences, but meeting up in person was taking things to a whole different level, and they were both racked with nerves.

Standing at the airport waiting for her to walk out through the arrivals gate, Leon felt his stomach lurch every time someone came through. What if he didn't recognise her? What if there was no connection between them?

But as soon as Debra rounded the corner, he knew it was her and all his nerves evaporated into the late-summer Texan air. Debra had done all her crying during all the long-distance phone calls they'd shared over the summer. Now her face bore a huge smile as she swept Leon up into a hug as if she'd never let him go. 'My God, I can't believe you're my son,' she kept saying, looking in wonder at this fully grown 26-year-old man, trying to see inside to the two-year-old he'd once been.

During the week that followed, mother and son made up for lost time, catching up on each other's lives, finding out each other's likes and dislikes. They couldn't believe the number of things they had in common, from the odd mannerism to the same taste in food.

It's difficult to come sweeping into someone's life after missing out on so many things, and Debra knew she had to tread warily with Sabrina, who was naturally protective of her husband, and with Leon's adoptive family. There were moments of undeniable tension as they all struggled to adapt to the seismic change that had come about within Leon's family group, but also moments of such joy that she could hardly take it in. Meeting her grandchildren for the first time, she'd been overcome with emotion, knowing how many times she'd prayed for just this moment.

For the first time he could remember Leon was meeting someone who shared the same blood as him, and even after a few days had passed he still had moments when he couldn't believe it was all real. Friends who called by would stare in amazement from grandmother to grandson and exclaim about the similarity of their eyes. For Leon, it was a real jolt to witness the continuity that ran from mother to son to grandchildren – all united in a blood line that he'd never experienced before.

Even though his half-sisters and -brothers didn't come on that initial visit, by the end of the week Leon almost felt like he knew them, so much did Debra talk about them. They'd also been in touch by phone and Internet.

It was as if his whole life was opening up again, just from that one moment when he'd idly typed a name into a computer.

✳   ✳   ✳

Across the Atlantic, Tony was gradually getting used to the idea that he was a granddad, and that his eldest son was now back in his life.

'I always knew this moment would come,' his tearful mum had told him on the phone from Jamaica, where she now lived. 'I knew you'd find each other again one day.'

Tony also knew that, while it was an occasion for rejoicing, he also needed to employ a certain amount of diplomacy. His second son needed reassuring that just because Leon was technically the oldest, it didn't mean he'd lost his place in the family. Also, Tony was very aware of not treading on Leon's adoptive family's toes. He contacted them to say how grateful he was to them for bringing him up. He never wanted them to feel as if he was barging in and taking their son away from them. He knew all too well how that felt.

He and Leon began to make plans for a reunion in England in 2009. Tony wanted him to meet his half-brothers and -sister. Leon was also intrigued by the idea of going back to the country he'd been born into but never really lived in.

✳   ✳   ✳

For all three of the people at the centre of this reunion, life changed completely that night in July 2008, when Leon Bailey keyed two words onto a website. Little wonder they all see the Internet as a powerful force for good.

'I'm not a particularly religious person, but I prayed every day that I'd see Leon again, and have all my children together,' says Debra. 'When I contacted the adoption agency, they couldn't help me. But the Internet connected us back together in just moments. It's incredible.'

Tony agrees that the Net is an amazing tool for getting people in touch with those they've let slip away, and also for giving us a sense of perspective on our lives. 'The problem with human beings is that we're always looking at ourselves as the centre of the world,' says Tony. 'It's as though other people cease to exist as soon as they go off of our radar. Having people come back into your life after years away with their own stories about the lives they've been leading makes you realise it's a big old world out there, and life goes on even outside of us. That's an amazing thought.

'Plus, I found my son on through a website. You can't get much more positive than that.'

Leon is firmly of the opinion that, used the right way, the Internet is an incredible tool. 'I thought I'd be looking all my life to find my birth parents. I always had that worry in my head that something would happen to them before I had a chance to find them, and to fit together those missing pieces of the puzzle. I searched for years for them, and in the end they were just a click of a mouse away.'

CHAPTER SIX

'WE WERE MEANT TO BE TOGETHER'

'Remember Stuart Lott, you used to go out with?'

Rachel Stabler was glad her brother was on the phone so he couldn't see the way she started at the mention of that familiar name from the past. 'Ye-e-s,' she replied slowly, trying to keep her voice from betraying the sudden excitement that had flared up inside her.

'Well, he's been asking after you.'

Rachel's brother went on to explain that he'd been organising a school reunion, and had wanted to get hold of Stuart's brother, who'd been one of his old classmates. Seeing that Stuart was registered on the Friends Reunited website, he'd contacted him for his brother's number. And that's when Stuart had asked him to say hello, and whether he could have her email address, just to make contact again.

After she put the phone down that evening in February, 2002, Rachel sat for a while just gazing off into space – an unusual luxury for the busy mother-of-four. It had been 22 years since she last saw Stuart Lott, and yet she found she could still remember him more vividly than some people she'd seen just last year, or the year before.

As 13-year-olds at school in Bournemouth, they'd gone out with each other for a while, in the casual way you did at that age. Rachel, who'd never had a huge circle of friends at school, just one or two close ones, remembered him as a lovely guy, the kind who'd do anything for you. Very different from the next boy she'd gone out with, who'd basically bullied her into ditching Stuart for him. Though she didn't know it at the time, this kind of threatening, abusive behaviour would set the pattern for most of Rachel's adult relationships.

She remembered, with a stab of regret, how ghoulish classmates had surrounded her on the day she'd dumped Stuart, shrieking: 'Oh my God, Stuart's *crying*!'

As soon as she finished with the bullying boyfriend, she'd sought Stuart out to try to explain why she'd acted as she had. By this time they were no longer at the same school but she still felt so bad for what had happened. All Stuart had ever done was be nice to her. She knew his family; their brothers were friends. She didn't want there to be bad feeling between them.

As usual, Stuart was kind and understanding. It was OK, he told her. He'd moved on. After that Rachel herself had moved away from the area, and that was the last time she'd seen him, although she'd thought about him from time to time. Sometimes when she'd been chatting to mates about first boyfriends, she'd had a clear image of the way he'd looked the last time she saw him, his warm smile and clear blue eyes, but she'd never dwelled on it too long.

With hindsight, Rachel could see she'd always subconsciously thought Stuart was too good for her. As a child she'd suffered horrific sexual abuse, which had left her with an ingrained mistrust of people and dangerously low self-esteem. Deep inside, she could see now, she'd felt she wasn't worthy of being treated well. Stuart was from a lovely family, he was nice to her – she simply didn't feel she'd deserved him. So when the other boy had come along, threatening her unless she split up with Stuart, she'd felt she didn't have much choice. This was her lot in life, she believed. She was good for nothing else.

In the intervening two decades not much had changed. Rachel had gone on to have a succession of abusive relationships with domineering men. She came to believe that the legacy of the sexual abuse she'd suffered as a child was that she gave off vulnerable signals that attracted a certain type of man – usually broken men who needed 'fixing'. She'd fix them up and they'd go on their way, leaving her behind to pick up the pieces. The result was that, at 37, she was a single mother to three children, living in a council house near Crawley and just about scraping by on benefits.

For the last couple of years though, she'd made a real attempt to get her life back under control. Through evening classes, she'd gained an AS level in photography and discovered a real talent for the subject. She was now hoping to go on to take a foundation course at college. For the first time in years, she had a real goal ahead of her, and was finally starting to feel good about herself. What she definitely, undoubtedly didn't need was another relationship. All that was behind her.

So when her brother told her he'd passed on her email address to Stuart, she didn't allow herself to get carried away with fairy-tale fantasies about how he'd come back into her life and sweep her off her feet. Even when Stuart sent her a first tentative email telling her about his life, how he was now divorced and had been on his own for three years, she deliberately ignored the flutter of excitement at seeing his name in her inbox.

But over the next couple of weeks, as Stuart's emails became more regular and intimate, Rachel's resolve started to weaken. He sounded so sincere in his emails, so down to earth and normal, especially after the emotionally insecure men she'd known in the past. And he had his life so sorted. He worked for a large advertising agency – one of the best in the country, he told her with pride – although he was currently on leave as he hadn't been too well. And he had a nice house in an upmarket village, big pension – the works. But when he gave her his phone number to call, she still hesitated. No matter how many times she told herself this was just an old friend re-establishing contact, she couldn't get around the fact that phoning Stuart would take things onto another level. Did she really want to make that move?

Rachel's heart was hammering when she finally got up the nerve to dial the number. It was about 10 o'clock in the evening and she'd finally got the children to bed. He probably wouldn't answer, she told herself. She'd leave a message and be in bed by 10.30.

In the event, that first conversation lasted six long hours. It was four in the morning when Rachel finally hung up, her head spinning. In bed, she lay awake going their conversation, unable to believe how easy it had been to talk to Stuart and how much they'd had in common, even after all these years.

But still, she told herself, she wasn't going to get involved. She'd explained to Stuart on the phone that she wasn't ready for a face-to-face meeting. It was wonderful talking to him on the phone, but she couldn't run the risk of meeting up with him. What if history just repeated itself? She'd had enough of men, had enough of relationships. Her life was just getting back on track.

At the time he'd said he understood and yet, a few days after that initial conversation, in mid March of 2002, Rachel's phone rang. 'It's me,' came the now familiar voice. 'I'm at the bottom of your road.'

Nervous shock raced through her, but Rachel didn't have time to think. Instead, she burst through her front door and ran down the road towards the lay-by at the bottom. There, leaning against a flashy-looking car, sun glinting off the lenses of his dark glasses, was Stuart.

He was just as she remembered him.

It had all happened too quickly for Rachel to pay heed to the warning voices in her head, which had told her not to get involved, urged her to move slowly.

'Fancy a drive?'

She climbed into Stuart's car, noting how new it was, as opposed to her own scruffy old motor. They drove around, chatting just as easily as they had over the phone, although there was an undercurrent of anticipation it was difficult to ignore. When they pulled up outside a park and Stuart leaned across and kissed her, it felt so natural, she pushed her misgivings aside. It sounded so clichéd but surely when something felt this right it was worth taking the risk?

When Stuart dropped her back at her house, Rachel didn't invite him in, but she did proffer an invitation: 'It would be nice if you came to take me out every now and then.'

Even though she'd been so wary, and so adamant she wasn't going to get involved again, Rachel just couldn't help falling for Stuart over the following weeks. He was so attentive, so considerate. She was wary about introducing him to her children, but in the event they loved him. Similarly, both her family and his were thrilled that they had found each other again, saying they'd never seen either of them so happy.

Stuart knew about Rachel's childhood abuse, and made it his mission to help her come to terms with it, taking her back to the hillside opposite where she used to live and gently talking her through all that had happened until it felt like all the bad stuff that had gone on in Rachel's life was melting away.

So when, just a few weeks after they met, Stuart asked her to marry him, she couldn't help but say yes. After all, they'd known each other over twenty years – it wasn't really as if they were rushing into anything. 'We should have been together always,' Stuart told her. 'We've wasted enough time. Let's do it straight away. It's just unfinished business, isn't it?'

Of course, after two failed marriages, there was a little sensible voice inside Rachel warning her to be careful, but she buried it deep down. She, like everyone around them, was swept away by the romance of the situation –

two soul mates who'd been parted for two decades had now found each other again. She knew she'd been a poor judge of character in the past, but this was her chance to put things right. And every time she had doubts, all she had to do was look at Stuart's face, and they crumbled away. She just knew they were going to be together forever.

So sure was she that she had a tattoo done of Stuart's name, spelled out in Japanese letters. It was an indelible symbol of their love – her way of proving to him, and to everyone else, that this relationship was going to be for life.

Nine weeks after they were first reunited, Stuart and Rachel were married, to the delight of their respective families. Looking up at her new husband, Rachel felt a rush of happiness. This time nothing would go wrong. She would make sure of it.

And for a while, it really did seem like the fairy tale was coming true. Stuart had moved in with Rachel as his own house was rented out, and he soon became an integral part of the family, helping the kids with the homework, doing the cooking and nursing Rachel with endless patience and gentleness whenever she had one of her migraines.

She did find it strange that he never seemed to go into work, but then he explained that he'd been ill. And he still had the car and the house and the big pension, so Rachel wasn't too worried that she seemed to be supporting him as well as her own family. But after a few weeks, she started to become aware of niggling details about Stuart that didn't seem to make sense. Like the way he never used any of his credit cards, but instead walked around with a cheque book all the time. Who used a cheque book these days? It seemed so odd. And why had he changed his name on all the official documents?

'It's because of my bitch of an ex-wife,' he was always telling her. 'If I don't stop her, she'll take everything I've got. That's why I've put everything into a different name.' Rachel would nod sympathetically, but still she wasn't entirely sure she understood.

Then there was the fact he never seemed to get any post, or any phone calls. It seemed so strange when he had property and all this money tied up in different places.

'Oh, my lawyer deals with everything,' Stuart told her evasively.

'So ring your lawyer then,' Rachel suggested. 'Just to check everything's OK.'

Only when he'd dialled the number and chatted to his lawyer in front of her, was she able to relax a little. She had to stop being so suspicious, she told herself sternly. Just because she'd been involved with men in the past who'd let her down, it didn't mean it was going to happen again.

But then came a knock on the door. There was a man

standing there on the doorstep, thin mouth set in an unsmiling line, waving some official papers around.

'It's about the car,' he told her.

At first Rachel couldn't understand what he was saying to her, and even when she did understand, she couldn't make sense of it. Stuart's flashy car, the one he'd tried to impress her with when they first met, was about to be repossessed. Bewildered and still protesting there must have been a mistake, she'd had to raid what little savings she had to stop the guy driving off in it there and then.

Stuart was full of excuses and explanations. He'd been off work longer than he expected, he told her. He'd pay her back as soon as he started earning properly again. And yet, when he did get another job, it was short-lived. And so was the next one. And the one after that. He didn't seem to be able to hold down a job, and in the meantime, he was on and off the dole. It wasn't quite how she'd envisaged her new married life.

Back at Rachel's house, the bills started to mount up. Stuart seemed to have run up a frightening amount of debt while he was out of work. His house was rented out, but the rent seemed to be eaten up by the mortgage every month, so they never saw a penny.

'You're going to have to cash part of your pension,' Rachel told him eventually. 'I know you don't want to, but it's big enough you can take some out and still have plenty left for when you retire. We've got to start paying off some of these bills.'

Stuart promised her he would, but said it might take time to release the money. That sounded reasonable enough. Rachel knew you couldn't just withdraw huge sums of money like that without any notice. But when weeks, and then months went by without any sign of the cash, she became increasingly anxious.

'Call your lawyer again,' she urged him.

Several times, she sat anxiously watching him while he dialled the number and held long, involved conversations about the money.

'It's on its way,' he'd promise her. And yet it never appeared.

Finally, after six months of nagging, Stuart cracked. 'I've got to tell you the truth,' he told her, unable to meet her eyes. 'There is no pension. I wanted to impress you. It was just because I loved you so much.'

Rachel gasped. She felt like someone had driven a punch right into her guts. Hard. All those lies. All those months he'd let her believe everything was going to be OK. And all the time he'd known the truth.

'Please forgive me,' he begged her, seeing the dawning horror on her face as she took in all the implications. 'I just said it because I wanted you to love me, and because I so wanted this marriage to work.'

Inside her reeling head, Rachel kept going through all

the times he'd looked her in the eye and told her something he knew to be a lie, the times he'd phoned a fictitious lawyer in front of her and had a one-sided conversation to a dialling tone. And yet she could see how contrite he was. And she reasoned his lies had come from insecurity, rather than malice. Besides, he was her husband.

'Look, I love you,' she told him, eventually giving way as he'd known she would. 'You don't have to make things up to impress me. I love the person you are. You don't have to pretend to be rich. I don't care about any of that.'

For a while after that, things were OK. Stuart had work and was bringing in some money to pay off some of the bills. The rest of the money, he borrowed from relatives and friends.

'Don't worry, I'll pay it back once I sell my house,' he promised her, after she'd grown upset at him borrowing from her brother. But Rachel was still uneasy. In all the years she'd been struggling as a single mother, she'd never once borrowed from other people. Ridiculous though it might seem, it had become a point of honour with her. Finally, after months of hassling him, he promised to put his house on the market to release some much-needed capital and pay off some of these rapidly accumulating loans.

But when Rachel started trying to pin him down on

dates and specific amounts, she had another shock. Again unable to meet her eyes, he told her the truth with his gaze fixed firmly on the carpet. The house wasn't his. He'd been renting it from a landlord when she'd first met him. Once again he confessed he'd lied to try to win her admiration.

Her new husband, it transpired, was completely and utterly broke.

But still Rachel couldn't bring herself to give up on him. Partly it was because she'd been married twice before. She was desperate to make a success of it this time. She didn't want to be the woman with four failed marriages behind her. And partly it was because she still loved Stuart. Money aside, he was still so kind and considerate and funny. The kids had all grown to care about him deeply, and together they felt like a proper unit. Then there were the two families – Rachel had always loved Stuart's family, and her own had taken him to their hearts like the long-lost son he practically was. How could she destroy all of that?

And so she decided to give him another chance. But this time no more lies, no more trying to impress her. Stuart agreed to everything she said. He loved her so much, he told her. All he wanted was to prove to her that he was a good man, a good husband and father.

Once again, he threw himself into showing her how sorry he was – helping around the house, taking the children to see their friends, looking after them while she started her photography course. When he was working, the money came in and some of the ever-growing mountain of bills was paid off. He was always magnanimous when he was earning, always wanting to appear generous, as well as prosperous.

One day, he came home and told Rachel that he'd won a draw at work and the prize was a day out in a classic Aston Martin. Coincidentally, her dad, who'd been recently diagnosed with cancer, had always dreamed of driving an Aston Martin. 'It'll be great,' Stuart told her excitedly. 'I'll take him out for the day, and we'll drive down to Cornwall and go to Rick Stein's restaurant.'

When Rachel broke the news to her dad, he was every bit as thrilled as they'd hoped, his spirits, low after the diagnosis, suddenly buoyed up in anticipation. Every few days, he'd ring Rachel to find out if the date for the car had been finalised yet. He was more excited than one of the kids, she joked. But as the weeks went by, Stuart stopped mentioning the car competition.

'I can't keep badgering them,' he'd tell her. 'It'll happen when it happens.'

Rachel's dad still phoned, with that tell-tale tone of hope in his voice, but less often, and then finally he stopped calling at all. The great prize had disappeared from their lives, just as suddenly as it had arrived – yet another of Stuart's grand promises that appeared, when you tried to grab hold of it, to vanish into thin air.

All too often now, Stuart wasn't working, and they'd struggle again, scratching around to find the money just to survive. But as long as they steered clear of the subject of finances, Rachel and Stuart still had a loving relationship. He was so romantic, almost slushy, it was impossible to stay cross with him for long. With the children, he was patient and thoughtful, knowing what to say whenever one of them had problems with friends or schoolwork. Only one incident gave her cause for concern.

Rachel's youngest daughter's beloved pet hamster had something wrong with its eye. 'Don't worry, I'll take it to the vet for you,' Stuart promised her. But instead, while the kids were at school, Stuart took the little squirming creature to the end of the garden and hurled it against the side of the shed as hard as he could.

'We can't afford vet bills,' he explained to a horrified Rachel.

She knew he was right, and yet she couldn't believe this gentle, sensitive man could have done something like that, and then lied so easily to her daughter, saying the vet had had to put the hamster down. That night, not for the first time, she sat watching Stuart's familiar face and wondered whether she actually knew him at all.

By the end of the fourth year of marriage, the couple's

financial situation became critical. Stuart hadn't worked for a little while and there was no income. But he told her he had a job lined up, so there was little point in starting the lengthy process to get assessed for state benefit. Instead, they lived on the child benefit Rachel received for the children, while Stuart went back and forward to London for meetings and interviews for this new job. 'It's going to be a big one,' he assured her. 'Our money problems will be over.'

When he heard he'd got the job, she felt shaky with relief. At last they could start planning for the future again. She took him to the station every morning, wincing at spending the little money they had on petrol when the kids were going without so many essential things, but knowing it was only a short-term problem. 'I can't wait for you to get your first month's wages,' she told him. 'At least we'll be able to do a proper supermarket shop at last.'

But when payday came and went without any sign of a payment, alarm bells started to ring. 'Bloody useless accounts department,' Stuart fumed. Snatching up the phone, he called to complain to someone and was assured his money would be transferred immediately.

So they waited... and they waited...

Finally, Rachel voiced the unthinkable. 'There is no job, is there?' she asked him.

Stuart started to protest, and then slowly shook his

head. He'd made the job up to please her. He'd been going to the library straight from the station, he told her, and staying there until it was time to come home. All the money she'd spent on petrol, that could have bought the kids food or new clothes, had been for nothing.

It was the final straw.

'I'm sorry, but nobody compromises my kids,' she told him.

The thought of going through another break-up, another failure was almost too much to contemplate. Despite everything, part of her still loved him – or at least loved the fairy-tale ending he'd once represented. And her kids were still so attached to him. But he'd let her down once too often. Plus, she knew only too well that the only way she could get any money was to register once again as a single parent. Stuart would have to go.

At first Stuart was beside himself, begging to be given another chance. He knew he'd messed up, he told her. But he'd done it all for her, for them. They were made for each other, weren't they? What about all that shared history? Surely being childhood sweethearts must count for something? But this time Rachel had had enough. Whatever happened, her children came first. Stuart had cynically deceived her – and them. She just couldn't afford to give him any more chances.

So, at the end of 2005, Stuart left. But not before

he'd helped himself to everything he wanted from Rachel's house.

That period following his departure passed in a blur. Naturally, the kids were distraught. They'd come to look on Stuart as a father figure, and suddenly he was gone. Some nights, when she curled up in bed on her own, Rachel would look at her tattoo, spelling out his name, and sob with pain and disbelief. She'd loved him so much. How could it have ended up like this?

In college the following week she had a major presentation to do as part of her degree, but she found herself in such a state, she didn't know if she could carry it through. 'Please can someone else go first,' she begged her tutor. Swapping with the next person in line bought her half an hour of time. 'Come on,' she urged herself. 'Don't fall apart now. Don't let that bastard do this to you.' By reminding herself of everything he'd already taken from her, and telling herself she couldn't allow him to take any more, she managed to stagger through the presentation, but inside she was anything but OK.

Rachel assumed Stuart had gone to stay with his parents, but by this stage she didn't really care. She just tried to get on with her life, clearing up the financial nightmare he'd left her with.

But a few weeks later, Stuart was back, looking thin and pale. 'I know you're angry with me, but please, just listen to me,' he begged her. 'I don't know what to do, or who else to turn to. I've just been diagnosed with Hodgkin's lymphoma. I'm so scared.'

Rachel was completely wrong-footed. All logical reason was telling her not to believe him, and yet the fear on his face was so real. What if he was telling the truth? What if he really did have cancer? She was still his wife – could she really turn her back on him?

'Look, if you're really ill, I'll support you,' she told him guardedly. 'When's your next hospital visit? I'll come with you.' When Stuart refused to tell her, and left suddenly, Rachel assumed he was lying as usual. But then two weeks later he was back, looking even worse than before.

'I'm so terrified,' he repeated.

In the face of his obvious distress, Rachel's conviction faltered. He looked so awful. Surely not even Stuart would lie about something like this? Awkwardly, she tried to comfort him. His body was rigid, and his eyes, when he turned them to her, were dazed and full of questions. His usual self-assuredness seemed to have completely deserted him. If ever there was a man who looked like he was facing a huge life crisis, it was Stuart.

After he'd gone, Rachel was thoughtful. In spite of everything that had happened, Stuart was still her husband, and a little stubborn part of her still loved him. If he was suffering from a potentially fatal illness, she wanted to be there for him. But how would she know?

She decided to go to see her GP, who looked after both she and Stuart and knew them both as a couple. She knew the GP was bound by confidentiality, but at least he should be able to tell her whether Stuart had been to see him recently.

Sitting in the waiting room, she didn't know what news she was most dreading – that Stuart did have cancer, or that he'd made it up. Immediately, she reprimanded herself. Of course she'd be relieved if Stuart didn't turn out to have a life-threatening illness.

But when the doctor shook his head, and told her Stuart hadn't been in to see him for a long while, her heart dropped within her ribcage. This wasn't just a case of Stuart lying to get out of a difficult situation or to impress her. She began to think he really was sick – only not in the way he'd tried to convince her.

Back at home, she called his parents. Although she'd always got along with them very well, she'd hardly spoken to them at all in recent years. They didn't want to hear her complain about their son, and besides she'd never been too sure what Stuart had been telling them about her. But she had to know for sure whether he was really ill.

By the time she put the phone down, she was more shaken than she'd been in a long time. 'He's had stomach cancer,' she'd been told. Apparently Stuart had even been to see his family wearing a bandage around his stomach. Something was clearly terribly wrong with the man she'd loved so fiercely, the man she'd thought was going to be her rock for the rest of her life.

Rachel set about researching Stuart's behaviour. The endless lies, the self-aggrandisement, the inability to recognise the effects of his actions on everyone around him. The description she kept coming back to was narcissism – a personality disorder where an individual believes so strongly in their own self-importance and advanced abilities, and has such an excessive need for admiration that they invent circumstances that either make them the centre of attention or make them appear to have achieved much greater things than is actually the case. The inability to empathise with others, also a facet of the disorder, prevents them from understanding how their fantasies might impact on the people close to them.

The more Rachel read about the disorder, the more she believed she recognised Stuart in the description. It explained so much – why he was so desperate for her to believe he was wealthy and successful, even though it was obvious she'd discover the truth eventually.

When Rachel heard soon afterwards that he'd been admitted to a local psychiatric institution, she was relieved. Maybe finally he'd get some help. He was such a great guy in so many ways, if he could just overcome this need for adulation and attention, he'd be the man she'd thought he was all along – strong, funny, so charming.

But a week later, Stuart was out again. Clearly, either he or the medical staff didn't believe he had a problem. Rachel soon discovered that he'd moved in with a woman in a nearby town, just a few miles away. It didn't take long for her to realise he must have had this woman lined up all along, even while he was begging her to have him back. She knew she was better off without him, and that she ought to be feeling sorry for this new woman. But it still hurt. Stuart had been her happy ending, the one who was supposed to sweep into her life on a charger and make all the bad things OK. And yet the more she discovered about him, the more she realised she'd never really known him.

For example, she learned from his family that while he'd still been married to his ex-wife, he'd not only had an affair with another woman, he'd also got engaged to her! In common with the text-book cases of narcissism, he seemed to be endlessly capable of believing in his own fantasies, his own hyperbole about himself. That was why he'd never thought through what would happen when his deceptions were uncovered. In his own mind, he was this glorious, high-achieving man who rescued vulnerable women and accepted their admiration and adoration as his due.

His family was understandably worried about him, but still Rachel was sure they didn't know the extent of his self-delusions. And as she had no idea of what stories he'd fabricated to them about her, she once again allowed contact to lapse.

Time passed without further word of Stuart, and Rachel tried to get her life back on track, looking into doing a degree course in fine art. But just as she was beginning to see some light at the end of the tunnel, she received a Christmas card from Stuart's parents. They hadn't heard anything from him for ages, they told her. They were worried about him. Did she know where he was? Could she check he was all right?

Of course, Rachel knew exactly where he was – shacked up with a new woman down the road from the house that they'd once shared together. Just leave it alone, she told herself. You don't owe him or his family anything. But now a seed of doubt had been planted in her mind. What if he was in some kind of trouble? Against her own better judgement, she found herself putting on her coat and setting off to find him.

It was a traditional chocolate-box-type neighbourhood, the kind that features heavily on English heritage websites and in sentimental films. The house was easy enough to find, as Rachel's car, which Stuart had taken, was parked outside – a tiny, but picturesque and beautifully maintained cottage. As Rachel walked nervously up the path, she couldn't help feeling a tiny stab of resentment as she compared it to her own far less well-tended home.

The woman who answered her tentative knock on the

door was much older than Rachel, but very glamorous and expensively groomed. As soon as she saw her visitor's face, she realised who she was and graciously invited Rachel to come inside.

The interior of the cottage was in keeping with the outside, with tasteful décor and subtle lighting. There was music playing softly and the table was formally laid as if guests were expected any minute.

As Rachel stepped inside, there was a heavy footfall on the narrow staircase and all of a sudden Stuart appeared, doing up his cuff links.

'What the hell are you doing here?'

It was all too much. The harshness of Stuart's tone, the cosiness of the cottage. All of a sudden, Rachel felt overcome. She shouldn't have come. It was a mistake. She turned and, yanking open the door, hurried down the path, flinging herself into the driver's seat of her own shabby-looking car. Seconds later, there was a gentle tap on the window. The well-dressed woman was standing by the side of the door, looking at Rachel with genuine concern.

'Do you want to talk?' she asked. Rachel shook her head numbly, and the woman turned to go back into the house.

Then it was Stuart's turn to come out. For a few moments, the two eyed each other wordlessly.

'You've landed on your feet,' Rachel said eventually.

Stuart had the good grace to smile ruefully. 'I'm sorry about everything that happened,' he told her. 'I've been working on myself, trying to work out what went wrong.' He looked so sincere, so full of good intentions, that for a moment Rachel found herself softening towards him in spite of everything. Then she remembered the position he'd put her in and the hurt on her children's faces when they'd realised he wasn't coming back again. The truth was, she realised, she'd never fully understand why Stuart had done the things he'd done, or why. And that was because she'd never really known him. Their shared history, the shared past, was a myth upon which they'd built a whole fairy-tale dream. As she drove home, she realised that remembering the same teachers and sharing some of the same teenaged memories didn't automatically create some magical unbreakable bond.

The next time she drove through the village where Stuart now lived, Rachel noticed that the picturesque little cottage was up for sale. Clearly, Stuart was on the move again. She was glad. This time she hoped she wouldn't ever see him again. This time, she was determined the past would stay past.

She threw herself back into studying, coming out with a first-class university degree, then went on to do a Masters, trying all the time to ignore the panic and anxiety that she'd felt ever since Stuart had gone. She'd come to feel so unsafe in her own skin.

Then, out of the blue, it all came crumbling down. All of a sudden she couldn't seem to cope with it any more, the crushing disappointment of it all: once again she'd been let down; once again love had turned out to be a con, a hollow façade with nothing at its centre.

In the autumn of 2008 Rachel suffered a breakdown and it was only when she'd come through it that she realised she'd never be able to make sense of what had happened. She had to just draw a line under it. She knew she couldn't afford to see a pattern emerging, it was just another unlucky thing, in a series of unlucky events, she told herself. It wasn't personal. But she knew it would be a long time before she ever trusted anyone again.

'There's a danger that you invest people from your past with a certain magic,' says Rachel now. 'Somehow you imagine that knowing each other as children means they'll always put your best interests at heart.

'Unfortunately it doesn't always turn out that way.'

CHAPTER SEVEN
REVENGE.COM

Whoever said 'revenge is a dish best served cold' would doubtless have approved of social networking sites, which provide the tools for disgruntled exes to get their own back without leaving the comfort of their own sofas, as these two accounts – with all names changed to protect the innocent – attest...

'NOW WHO LOOKS STUPID?'

The moment he saw the car parked up, with the two figures inside, Simon P knew it was bad news. He recognised one immediately – Suzanne, his on-off girlfriend and the mother of his little girl. The other, he now realised, was a friend of his, a policeman.

Simon's head was pounding as he parked his own car and walked slowly over to the other vehicle. He just didn't get it. He and Suzanne had been apart for so long, he'd long ago learned to accept their separation, despite having once loved her to pieces and been desperate to stay together. When she'd made it clear she didn't see any future for them, he'd reluctantly learned to push her to the back of his mind and pick up the pieces of his life, even meeting another woman who seemed to genuinely care for him. But lately he'd really had the opinion she wanted to make it work again, to be a family again for the sake of their daughter. So what was all this about?

As he approached the other car, Suzanne finally recognised him, and the expression on her face was far from welcoming. 'Go away,' she hissed, flicking her long dark hair angrily. 'I don't want to see you.'

Simon's fingers were digging into his palms, but he tried to stay calm.

'I just want to talk to you,' he told her.

'Go AWAY!'

She wound the window up and turned her head, her jaw set in that clenched way he remembered so well. In the driver's seat, her male companion smirked at Simon in a way that might have been intended as sympathetic, but came across as mocking.

Simon felt his face burning, and a wave of fury swept through him, pushing out all rational thought in its wake. Too late he remembered all those times in the past Suzanne had evoked in him this same kind of impotent rage, and how relieved he'd been to finally leave all that behind him.

As he walked away from the car, he imagined what the two of them would now be saying about him, how they'd be ridiculing him, and he had to bite down on his lip to keep himself under control.

She hadn't really wanted him back after all, he decided. She'd just been jealous that he'd managed to build up a life without her. It was all a game with her – she didn't want him, but she didn't want anyone else to have him either. After all these years, she was still playing her little power games. And, like the mug he was, he'd let her right back into his life.

Simon hoped that visiting the friend he'd been on his way to see would calm him down. But when he drove home later that evening, the image of what had happened earlier came back into his mind and his sense of outrage returned.

Almost from the start, as far as he could see, Suzanne had played him for a fool, but he'd been too blind, or too in love, to see it. When they'd first got together, five years before, there'd been a honeymoon period where everything had been okay, but as soon as their daughter was born, things had started to go wrong.

He'd felt he wasn't good enough for her any more. Things she'd said had made him feel stupid and inadequate. When she'd finally called time on their relationship, he'd been devastated, but in some ways it had come as a relief. At least now there'd be no more rows. He wouldn't wake up every morning worrying about what kind of mood she'd be in, or go to bed wondering where he stood.

Suzanne blamed him for the split, saying he was unreasonable and impossible to live with, but he had his own suspicions about why she wanted to be on her own.

Soon after they broke up, she started seeing someone else – a banker. 'She's finally got what she wanted,' he'd tell friends bitterly. 'Someone with money.'

There was a period after the break-up when Simon struggled to accept the relationship was really over. He'd thought they were a family, that they were happy together. Sure, they'd had their share of arguments, but he'd never stopped loving her. Unable to take no for an answer, he kept trying to talk to her, certain there must be some way to make her see she was making a mistake. In the end, it took a warning from the police to convince him that she really didn't want anything more to do with him. Even though it was tearing him up inside to realise they'd never be a family again, he had to keep away from her.

For the sake of their daughter, the couple had to stay in touch, but they tried to keep contact to a minimum and slowly Simon began rebuilding his shattered confidence. He met another woman, Tracy, someone who seemed to value him for who he was, who found him funny and attractive. He saw his daughter regularly, and though she sometimes came out with things that made him wonder exactly what her mother had been saying about him, like the time she sobbed that she didn't want him to die, he loved being a part of her life, treasuring the time they spent together.

But when Suzanne's new relationship faltered, some months after the initial separation, she started once again to move back into his life. First it was the odd text, more friendly in tone than the curt ones he'd been getting about the childcare arrangements. Then there were phone calls, and then she'd started dropping round to see him where he worked.

It had been too much for his new girlfriend. She'd broken things off. 'I can't compete,' she'd told him, resignedly. 'Suzanne will always have the trump card of being the mother of your child. I'll never really come first.'

Simon had been torn then. He'd really liked Tracy. In the short time he'd been with her, he'd already seen a different side to relationships. He saw how it was possible to be with someone else without a constant undercurrent of tension and the ever-present threat of arguments. And yet he and Suzanne had been through so much together. More than that, they shared a daughter together.

Didn't they owe it to each other to give it another go?

Even as they went through the initial stages of getting to know each other again, though, Simon could sense something wasn't right. When they were on their own, Suzanne gave him the impression she wanted him back. 'I've missed you so much,' she'd tell him. Yet in public, she barely acknowledged him. She'd send him long, flirty texts, and then he'd find out she'd been 'talking' to other men on Internet dating sites.

At first, he made excuses to himself. After everything she'd said about him to family and friends, it would be hard for her to admit she was seeing him again. How would that make her look?

But then, word started filtering back to him that she'd been telling friends he was the last person she wanted to be involved with. 'She says the two of you aren't together at all, it's all in your head,' he was told. Within weeks he was right back to where he'd been just a few months before – going round in circles, not knowing what was real.

So when she'd refused to talk to him in that parked car, when he'd had to walk away with his hands bunched up in humiliation, something had snapped inside him. Driving home from his friend's house later that day, all the anger and the confusion of the last few months washed over him in one big tidal wave of emotion. Just what was she playing at? Why did she think she could do this to him?

Back home, he decided to have an early night and

hope that in the morning things would look brighter. But he found he couldn't sleep. Tossing and turning, he couldn't get the image out of his head of her in that car, his friend's smirking expression. She was so quick to hold him up to public ridicule. What would people say if they knew what she was *really* like? She wanted everyone to think she couldn't stand him – what would they say if they saw the photos she used to send him on her mobile of her naked or topless? Then they'd realise who was leading who on in this relationship.

That was when the thought crept into his head. Why shouldn't everyone see those photos?

Springing out of bed, he switched on his computer. It was the work of moments to upload the photos. Then he called up the Facebook website. He knew from experience how easy it was to create a new account: all you needed was a name and a few details – oh yes, and a few choice pictures...

She was making him a laughing stock, and she thought she could just get away with it. Well, she was wrong.

❋   ❋   ❋

Suzanne gazed at her computer screen, puzzled. She'd checked into her Facebook account as normal, but something wasn't quite the same. For some reason it seemed to be telling her that she now had a second account.

Clearly there'd been some kind of mix-up. She idly followed the prompted links. Then all of a sudden, she froze. There on the screen, magnified and agonisingly public, were all the photos she'd taken to send to Simon when they were in a happier time in their relationship – the ones she'd only ever meant for him to see.

'Oh my God,' she gasped. 'I don't believe it. How could he have done this to me?'

❋   ❋   ❋

Almost as soon as Simon had finished creating his false Facebook account in Suzanne's name, the first pangs of regret had started to creep in.

Should he really have done that?

Just before he'd finally got to sleep, he'd made a mental note to himself to do something about the page the following day. Luckily, it would take a while for anyone to spot it, so he still had time to retract it without anyone being any the wiser. For the time being, he'd just enjoy the rare feeling of having actually taken the lead for once – even if only he ever knew about it.

But the next day, he was awoken by a loud banging. Half asleep, he pulled open the front door to find two police officers standing on his doorstep. For a few seconds, he had no idea what they could be after, but then it all came flooding back to him.

'It wasn't... I didn't mean...'

There was nothing to say, no excuses. No amount of explanations could disguise the fact that he'd done exactly what he was being accused of doing. His moment of sweet revenge would end up costing him very dear.

In early 2008, Simon P admitted to a charge of harassment in front of a magistrate's court and was given a short, suspended jail sentence. He was also made the subject of a restraining order, meaning he can no longer go near his former partner – something he insists is actually the farthest thing from his mind.

He bitterly regrets his 'moment of stupidity' and accepts that even though the page was only active for less than 24 hours, it was enough to cause profound embarrassment and hurt. But he also thinks websites like Facebook have to take some sort of responsibility. 'It's so easy to do what I did,' he says. 'You could set up an account in the Queen's name if you wanted to. There are no checks. It's scary.'

And he's not the only one who's been on the wrong end of the social networking website phenomenon. 'So many of my friends have broken up because of it – because of something they've said, or because they've added a particular girl as their friend.

'Sites like that can destroy lives.'

'MAYBE YOU SHOULD CHECK
YOUR WEB PAGE...'

Just for the briefest moment, Paul R's fingertips hovered over the computer mouse. Eighteen inches away from him, the screen returned his gaze impassively, giving nothing away. The air in the room seemed suddenly so dense around him, it was almost tangible. In the balance hung everything: reputation, friends, even potentially his liberty. But on the other side was the one thing that outweighed everything else. Revenge.

With a tight feeling around his rib cage, he clicked the 'send' button.

It was done. There was no going back.

❊   ❊   ❊

Paul had been devastated when his 20-year-old girlfriend Nicole told him their relationship was over in May 2003. 'I really like you,' she'd told him in that time honoured way. 'But I don't think we're right for each other.'

Paul was distraught. Although they'd only been together for eight months, the 21-year-old student, in his final year of a university degree, had been smitten with his attractive girlfriend, and had been hoping they had some kind of future together. When she told him it was finished, he found it almost impossible to understand or accept.

'Give me another chance,' he begged. 'Please.' To his mind, things had been going so well. He just couldn't comprehend why she'd dumped him. Unless… unless… There must be someone else.

Paul was far from unique in needing to feel there was someone else involved in the end of his relationship. For many lovers, the existence of a third person provides a focus for all the anger and bitterness they might otherwise direct upon themselves. By blaming an outside party, they can preserve their relationship in their minds as something perfect and unsullied.

Usually this is a transient strategy, a way of coping with the most painful period just after a break-up, but for Paul the idea of the 'other man' became an obsession. There must have been someone else, he kept telling himself. Why else wouldn't she want to stay with him? None of it made sense unless she had someone else already lined up. His nagging suspicion began to drive him crazy. He had to know for sure.

'I can't do that!' Paul's friend exclaimed when he realised what was being asked of him.

'No one will ever find out,' Paul wheedled. 'I just want to set my mind at ease.'

Fond though they were of him, the two friends he'd approached were understandably reluctant to do the favour he was asking. They both worked for a mobile phone company and Paul was asking them to intercept messages from his ex-girlfriend's phone. They could lose their jobs. Or worse.

But Paul could be very persuasive. He just wanted to know the truth, he told them. Just to put his mind at rest. He'd do the same for them if the positions were reversed, he told them. Eventually – and with major misgivings – they agreed to help him.

❋   ❋   ❋

'OK, this is what you were looking for. For God's sake don't ever show it to anyone else.'

The handover was furtive. Awkward. The printout that was thrust into Paul's hand held a record of various mobile phone messages. Amazing how mundane most texts are... the endless practical arrangements, changes of shift times, meeting up for a keep-fit class, the last-minute food items that need picking up, the hangovers compared.

But in among the throwaway comments, the girly gossip and the boring everyday details of an ordinary life, Paul found what he had been looking for. Hidden away amidst the jokes and the time queries were the answers to the questions that had been tormenting him.

Nicole, it seemed, had rekindled a relationship with an old flame.

The fact that he'd been proved right didn't stop Paul from feeling winded, as if someone had slugged him in his solar plexus. Nicole had been his dream woman – gorgeous, vivacious and sexually open-minded. He couldn't believe she'd given him up, apparently for someone else.

Surely she could see how much they had in common? Surely she couldn't have been so short-sighted as to pass up everything they had for some other guy who probably wouldn't treat her half as well?

If Paul's feelings were injured, his pride was even more so. Like many people who believe their partner to be unfaithful, he found himself tormented by the idea of being made a fool of. How long had she been seeing this other man, he wondered? Had she been flirting with him, or worse, all the time they'd been together? Wretchedly, he ran past scenarios through his mind, rewriting them to fit in with this new potential reality. When she said she'd been doing X, had she secretly been doing Y? That time she'd been late... that weekend she'd been away...

All the time he'd foolishly been imagining their relationship to be strengthening, had she in fact been doing her best to undermine it, laughing behind his back with this other guy? And what about since the break-up? What things they'd done together was she now doing with this other man, this usurper? Was this other guy seeing all the parts of her Paul had thought his and his alone? What intimacies were they sharing? What private world had they created?

Before long, Paul's despair had turned to a primeval,

ungovernable anger and a desperate thirst for revenge. As far as he was concerned, Nicole had hurt him and made him feel, and look, stupid. Well, now she was going to find out just how that felt.

Public humiliation was what Paul had in mind – and he had just the means at his disposal. In his possession were exceedingly intimate videos of him and Nicole having sex, which were never intended to be seen by anyone apart from themselves. Well, now Nicole was about to get a far wider exposure than she'd bargained for.

Paul knew that Nicole had a profile page on the website Friends Reunited. With her username and password, it would be the work of minutes to post stills from the X-rated videos up on the site. What would all her old friends say, he wondered, if they saw the compromising pictures? They'd certainly see a side of their old classmate that might surprise them.

Before he went ahead, Paul sent Nicole a series of texts, dropping hints about the videos still in his possession. Did he think that he might somehow be able to blackmail her back into having a relationship with him? Or was he just so desperate for another chance to see her that he was prepared to use any excuse to engineer a meeting?

Whatever the case, the two former lovers met up again, but if he'd had hoped it might prompt Nicole to revive the relationship, he was bitterly disappointed. Instead, she was only interested in retrieving the videos.

'Don't worry. I'll give them back,' he assured her, handing them over. What she didn't know was that Paul had made copies.

✳   ✳   ✳

'You ought to have a look at your Friends Reunited page.' It was the tone of her friend's voice – concerned, shocked, angry – that made Nicole's insides freeze. With a feeling of trepidation, she turned on her computer and logged onto her profile page. Immediately, she felt sick. Posted up on the page, for everyone to see, were the most sensitive photos of her and her former boyfriend. She couldn't believe that her most private moments were being shared by any stranger who happened to follow the link to her page. Almost worse, all her friends and family would be able to see them as well.

Not only that, but Paul had changed the text in her profile. Shaking with shock and humiliation, she gazed open mouthed at the words she hadn't written, and the pictures she certainly hadn't posted, unable to believe that someone she'd trusted had betrayed her so cruelly.

But worse was still to come. He had also hacked into her email account. Another friend who'd sent her a message had found herself redirected to images on the Friends Reunited page. As if that wasn't enough, the vindictive scorned lover had set up another web page, which bore Nicole's own name in its URL. Nicole typed in the address with trembling fingers and waited while the site loaded. Everything seemed to go into slow motion – the clock on the computer, the noise of the traffic outside. But when the page finally loaded, she wished time had stayed frozen altogether: it contained the video footage Paul had told her would be seen by no one apart from themselves, that he'd convinced her he was handing over. As the grainy images filled the screen, she was assailed by a mixture of shame, anger, shock and total disbelief.

The thought that people she didn't know could be clicking onto to see her in the kind of way only the most trusted of lovers ever should made her feel exposed and degraded, as if she'd been suddenly turned into public property for strangers to paw at.

Paul had got his moment of revenge. But it came at a price.

After a distressed Nicole contacted police, he was taken in for questioning. A search of his Surrey home revealed a stack of X-rated posters of his ex girlfriend, taken from the same video tapes, which the student had planned to put up around Nicole's home town.

In December 2003, Paul R pleaded guilty to unlawfully obtaining personal data, unauthorised modification of a computer program and harassment. A judge sentenced him to five months' imprisonment and he was banned from Friends Reunited. The two friends he'd enlisted as accomplices were sacked and fined.

When Nicole put up her details on Friends Reunited, she intended to give a few old friends a general update on her life, but she ended up sharing with total strangers some of her most intimate and most private moments.

In the right hands, a social networking site can be an invaluable instrument for reconnecting and disseminating information. In the wrong hands, it can become a perfect vehicle for revenge.

CHAPTER EIGHT
BLOOD BROTHERS

ummer in New York City. Outside, the heat was rising off the pavements in a steamy mass, causing sluggish pedestrians to seek out the shade of shop awnings and tall buildings, making occasional forays into the larger stores and office blocks where the sudden shock of the air-conditioning caused them to stop for a moment on the threshold to reacclimatise.

Back home at his family's apartment in Queens for the summer, medical student Karl Celestine sat in front of the computer, curtains drawn against the relentless sun, idly messaging his old friends to let them know he was around and to fix up a few nights out. For most of the year, Karl lived in the Dominican Republic, where he was partway through a course in medical school. The same course would have cost over $100,000 dollars to complete in the

US, but by opting to study in the tiny Caribbean country, which shares an island with Haiti, the tuition fees were slashed to around a fifth. Karl loved the easy way of life on the island and the lazy afternoons on the white sandy beaches, but it was always exciting to be back home again, catching up with old friends, seeing all the little changes that the preceding months had wrought in the city, soaking up the energy that was New York.

Logging onto his Facebook account, Karl flicked his eyes over his newsfeed, noting which of the hundreds of friends he'd managed to acquire had been active online since his last session. Noticing the alert that told him he had new messages waiting, Karl clicked on his inbox. Suddenly he sat upright in his chair. There, in his 'unread mail' folder, was a name that he hadn't seen for so many years it took a few seconds for his brain to register. Ricardo Manier.

Immediately, there leapt into his mind an image of a lanky, smiling young boy, goofing around in front of a classroom of laughing children. Then, another image of the same boy and Karl himself, as he was ten years before, on a basketball court swapping high fives after a particularly memorable victory. But then came the other memories, of visiting a hospital where a very sick boy lay in bed, his face bloated, his eyes dull from pain and boredom. Karl remembered feeling slightly awkward as he stood in the hospital room, wishing there was something he could do to make his friend jump out of bed and become once again the class comedian they all knew and loved.

Ricardo, better known as Ricky had joined Karl's school – the Holy Family Elementary School in Fresh Meadows, Queens – when the two boys were around nine. Before that, Ricky had been living in Philadelphia, then California, moving around as his mother's interior-design career progressed. Luckily, he'd never had a problem making friends. Likeable and funny, he was one of those kids who settled in quickly wherever he was and he and Karl were soon buddies, going to boy scouts together and playing on the basketball team.

But there was something different about Ricky. From the age of five, he'd suffered from nephrotic syndrome – a rare kidney disease that in his case was associated with focal segmental glomerulosclerosis, or scarring on the kidneys. It meant the tiny blood vessels inside his kidneys were leaking, causing protein to pass from his blood into his urine and then out of his body. For as long as he could remember, Ricky's life had been split down the middle. Most of the time, he was a happy, popular, energetic boy who loved sport and being with his friends. But then his face would start getting puffy and he'd start gaining weight – up to 35lb of water retained in his body. He didn't want to eat, he'd feel tired and lethargic and often he'd end up in hospital, sometimes for a week, sometimes a month.

His new classmates at Holy Family School grew used

to Ricky's lengthy absences from the classroom. Sometimes lesson timetables would be altered so that the children could spend a class making cards to try to cheer him up during his long, often mind-numbingly tedious stays in hospital. Occasionally they'd even go to visit him, standing next to his bed, shifting their weight nervously from foot to foot, casting anxious glances up and down the ward, trying hard not to stare.

Karl remembered how pleased they'd all be when he reappeared after these hospital stays. They'd come in to class and there he'd be, beaming away at them, looking so much back to his old self that it was impossible not to smile straight back, caught up in his infectious delight in being back in his ordinary life.

The boys were firm friends, soul mates even, until 1998 when, as both of them reached the age of 13, Ricky's family was once again on the move – this time to California. At the time it had been a big blow to Karl, losing one of his best friends. But at 13 it can seem like everything is changing all at once, and Ricky's departure soon faded into the background as Karl began adjusting to life as a teenager in New York.

For a while, the two had stayed in touch, exchanging emails where they'd talk, in time-honoured boys' fashion about sport or school, rather than illness or – heaven forbid – anything emotional. But inevitably, as each developed separate and full lives with new friends and challenges, the email contact grew more sporadic. Ricardo, with his new Californian outdoors lifestyle, seemed like a world away from Karl, back in gritty New York and eventually, the correspondence petered out completely after four or five years.

Until now.

Fast forward to the summer of 2007, and there's Karl sitting at his computer in his stifling New York apartment, and getting a jolt when he sees that familiar name in his inbox. Eagerly clicking open the message, he read to his delight that his old school friend Ricky was once again back in New York City. But his excitement was tempered by concern when he went on to read that Ricky hadn't been feeling too well since being back in his old neighbourhood, and in fact he'd been in and out of hospital for weeks.

What Karl didn't know is that this time Ricky was seriously sick. It had happened so gradually that he had hardly been aware of it. He'd felt OK, but had started sleeping more and more – up to 18 hours a day.

'You don't look well,' his worried mother kept telling him.

Trouble was, he felt OK – until he developed a severe pain in his foot that was later diagnosed as gout. Once again, Ricardo found himself in hospital. Only this time, the news was worse than usual.

'How on earth are you still walking around?' the

incredulous doctor asked Ricky, waving the results of his latest blood test in his hand. The hospital had assessed Ricky's kidney function by measuring the amount of creatinine in his blood. Creatinine is a chemical that is a waste product of muscles in the body and high levels indicate that the kidneys aren't filtering waste as they should. At 15.9, Ricky's levels weren't just dangerously high: they were well-nigh impossible. 'Another week or so without treatment and you'd have been dead,' warned the doctor.

There was only one possible course of treatment: dialysis. Ever since he was a child, Ricardo and his mum had known he'd have to have dialysis one day, but they'd been hoping to put it off as long as possible. Unfortunately, there was now no choice.

As the rest of New York eased its way into the long, hot summer, Ricardo began a new, agonising regime. Three times a week, he'd get up at 5am and make his way to the hospital, where he'd be connected up to a dialysis machine for hours on end, which would basically take over the job of his kidneys for a few hours, taking the blood from his vein and filtering it of waste, before returning it to his body. Ricky soon grew to dread the sight of the needles the size of nails, and the agonising hours spent lying there while the machine did its work. More than anything, he hated the knowledge that this would be his life from now on.

'Surely there has to be another option?' he asked his doctors.

'Only a kidney transplant,' he was told. 'And the waiting list in New York is ten years long.'

Only if Ricardo found a donor himself would there be any chance of him getting off the hated dialysis, and even then it was far from a sure thing, as the willing donor still had to be a good match in terms of blood types. It seemed impossible.

It was while Ricardo was in hospital on dialysis that he started spending long hours on the Internet, trying to make the time pass more quickly. Like many young people, he was a member of the mass social networking website Facebook. He'd amassed a sizeable list of 'friends' and he'd spend his time sending messages, or generally keeping up with what they were all doing. It was while he was browsing Facebook that he decided to try out the function enabling users to track down old schoolmates. Looking up Holy Family School, he was gratified to find so many of his former classmates listed there, all fellow Facebook members. Among the names was one that was very familiar: Karl Celestine.

With more time on his hands than he knew what to do with, Ricardo set about composing a message to Karl, bringing him up to date on the fact he'd now moved to New York and telling him a bit about what had been going on in his life. He told him he'd just finished pre-med school and had got a part-time job as a doorman, but because of being ill, he wasn't sure what was going to happen next.

Within hours, he had a reply. Karl was ecstatic to hear from him and to know that once again they were back in the same neighbourhood. 'When can we meet up?' he wanted to know.

Then Ricky had to bring his old friend up to speed on his new post-dialysis timetable – the three days a week he spent in the hospital, the agonising slowness with which the hours passed.

'What you need is a night out,' Karl decided after listening sympathetically. They arranged that Karl would come and pick Ricardo up one day after dialysis.

After so much time had passed they were curious whether they'd recognise each other, but as soon as Karl set eyes on the guy emerging from the hospital exit, he knew it was Ricky. Taller, skinnier, older, but undeniably the same grinning boy who'd had them all in stitches in the classroom all those years before. Only the paleness of his complexion, and the acne that covered his face, betrayed the fact that this was someone who was also gravely ill.

Over a few drinks, the two old friends caught up with everything that had been going on in each others' lives. Karl told an envious Ricardo all about medical school in the Dominican Republic, and Ricardo told Karl how he'd done his pre-med course but would struggle going on to further medical training because of being tied to dialysis three or four times a week. Under the terms of his health insurance, he had to remain in New York for his treatment.

Then Ricky described what the dialysis was like. Karl, who'd always counted himself lucky to be healthy, listened with growing distress at what his friend had to endure week in week out. 'Man, that sucks,' he told him, wishing there was something more comforting he could say or do.

From that day, Karl and Ricardo met up every day, often with another old school friend. They became like brothers, and it was soon as if the 'missing' decade of no contact had never happened.

One day, they were chatting as usual about this and that, when Ricky started talking about dialysis again, and saying that the only chance of getting out of it was to have a transplant. 'I've just got to wait for a kidney to become available,' he explained.

That evening, Karl went home and told his family over dinner what Ricardo had said. His deeply devout mother looked thoughtful. Then she spoke: 'You know,' she said to Karl, 'If you turn out to be a match for Ricky, you should offer to donate one of your kidneys.'

It was the first time that thought had even entered Karl's head, but as soon as his mum made the suggestion, he started thinking, *Why not?* After all, as a medical student himself, he knew enough to be aware this was no longer a particularly high-risk operation. Further research on the computer left him even more convinced. Why shouldn't he do it? Why shouldn't he help his friend?

The following day, the two men were driving to a club when Karl turned to Ricky. 'You know, if you need a kidney, I wouldn't mind giving you one,' he announced.

Ricardo was stunned. Ever since he'd started dialysis people had made vague noises about becoming a donor to try to make him feel better, but something about the way Karl looked at him made him realise he actually meant what he was saying.

'I'm serious, man,' Karl said, as if reading his friend's thoughts. 'I'll give you a kidney if you need it. After all, I've got two!'

Instinctively, Ricardo knew that if he accepted this offer, everything would change. He would owe this man his life. But weirdly, he didn't feel awkward or nervous. Instead, he and Karl talked about it quite calmly and normally, as if they were discussing a forthcoming ball game rather than a major life-saving operation.

After a while, Ricky turned to Karl with a slight grin on his face. 'All right,' he said lightly. 'Let's do it.'

But just because Karl had made the offer, didn't mean the operation was necessarily in the bag. Despite feeling like brothers, the two men weren't related and there was no guarantee they'd be a match. Both tried to downplay any expectations or excitement, for fear of being disappointed.

At the end of August 2007, Ricardo made an appointment with his doctor to get his own blood and Karl's tested. 'Whatever happens, I want to thank you for doing this,' he told his friend. There followed an agonising two-week wait until the results of the test were known. During that tense fortnight, the two men attempted to focus on other things, trying to distract their minds from dwelling too much on what might or might not be about to happen. Then, finally, came the call. The results were in. Despite the fact that Ricardo's bood group was AB and Karl's O positive, there had been no negative reaction from the blood test.

'Congratulations,' the doctor told them both. 'You're a perfect match.'

Coming off the phone from the hospital, Karl's mind was surprisingly calm. He wasn't scared or worried, just resolved. *OK*, he thought to himself. *So it's really going to happen.*

The doctor had advised him to talk to his family about the results, so he called his mother. 'It's God's will,' was her response.

Ricardo's reaction was slightly more upbeat. 'I'm so excited,' he exclaimed down the phone, hardly daring to believe that the days of dreaded dialysis might really be numbered.

But not everyone was so positive. Karl found that some of the people he'd thought would be most supportive counselled him against going ahead with the operation. His father and many of his friends couldn't see past the fact that he was voluntarily putting himself under the knife. 'It's an organ,' his dad told him – as if Karl, a medical student, hadn't already worked that out. 'You're going to have it taken out of your body. It's too risky.'

But by this time, Karl had done all his research. He knew that advances in medical technology meant the transplant operation was a lot less traumatic than in previous times. He reminded himself that these doubters were acting out of a combination of concern for him and ignorance about the reality of the situation. Now that he'd committed to this, he was determined that nothing was going to put him off going through with it.

Karl went back to the Dominican Republic to begin the new school year, trying to put the thoughts of the forthcoming operation out of his mind while he focused on his studies. But at the end of January 2008, he found himself back in New York being put through a barrage of tests to make absolutely sure that he and Ricardo were a match, and that nothing should go wrong. Only once the doctors were convinced the operation had every chance of success were they given a date for surgery: 28 February 2008.

When Karl once more flew back to New York at the

end of February, he was amazed at the reception he received. Somehow word had got out about the two reunited friends who were about to undergo life-saving surgery. Newspaper and television journalists wanted to know how they'd come to find each other again, what each felt about the forthcoming surgery, how their families had reacted to it all.

Time and time again, they were asked the same questions: how had they found each other again? Were they nervous about what was going to happen? They grew warily accustomed to the flashbulbs going off in their eyes and the clicking of tape recorders.

'It's not such a big deal,' Karl kept repeating, his fingers picking nervously at the seam of his jeans. 'I'm just a friend helping out another friend. Anyone would have done the same.'

At first, he found the attention invigorating – all these people showing an interest in him, as if he was doing this amazing thing. But after a while, he started to get annoyed with it. Why should it be such a big story just because someone was helping someone else? Surely it should be the norm rather than the exception? He grew irritated with the questions, and the endless photos. He just wanted to get this whole thing over with.

The day before the surgery was inevitably underscored with tension, although the two men tried their best to play down what was happening. In the evening, they both took their girlfriends and their mums, who by that time had become good friends, to the home of Ricardo's grandmother, where they all sat around talking and laughing, and trying not to think too much about what was about to happen.

But by five o'clock the following morning, the time they were due at the hospital, there was no possibility of ignoring it any longer. As they made their way to the ward, the two men drew strength from each other's proximity. Knowing that they would be going through this ordeal side by side somehow made the whole thing less frightening.

Karl would be the first to have his operation. As he sat in his hospital gown, waiting to go into surgery, with his mum and girlfriend close by him, the nerves really kicked in. This was a pretty major operation, after all. What if something went wrong? What if he reacted badly to the anaesthetic? What if Ricky's body rejected the kidney and it had all been in vain?

Making a huge effort to keep these thoughts suppressed, he kissed his girlfriend and his mum, then turned to Ricardo. 'Good luck, man,' he told him, their eyes saying everything their awkward goodbyes couldn't.

Then he was lying on the table in the surgery, looking up at the ceiling and the faces of the doctors and nurses. 'We're going to give you something to relax,' he was told. And then everything went black.

Ricardo, meanwhile, was still outside waiting for his turn to go in. Outwardly, he was handling everything just fine, laughing and chatting to his mum and passing medical staff. But inside his head he was battling a tide of conflicting emotions. He was anxious about his friend who was out there on an operating table undergoing invasive surgery on his behalf. He was nervous about his own operation – he knew the likelihood of complications, and the ever-present threat that his body could reject Karl's donated kidney. But underneath all this, there was another emotion – excitement. If this operation was successful it would be like having his life handed back to him, or rather a new life without the endless hospital visits, the pain, the worry of what the future would bring.

An hour after Karl's operation, while he was still unconscious, it was Ricky's turn to say his goodbyes to anxious well-wishers and make his way into the operating room. As he began his descent into unconsciousness, it was hard to avoid the thought that when he came to again, everything would have changed.

As Ricardo's operation, obviously far the more complex and dangerous, got underway, Karl was lying in the recovery room, surrounded by friends and family. His first thought as he began to regain consciousness was how cold he was. He could feel his body shivering, despite the weight of the blankets on top of him. Slowly he opened his eyes, blinking momentarily in the glare of the bright hospital light. When he finally focused, he could see a sea of familiar faces looking anxiously at him.

His mouth felt dry and uncomfortable as he opened it to speak: 'Hey, what's up?' As epic lines go, it wasn't the most impressive, but it had an immediate effect on those around him, who broke into universal smiles of relief. As Karl's bleary eyes scanned the room he could see that even those who'd initially been against him having the surgery were laughing. Although he was increasingly aware of pain in his muscles, Karl realised at that moment that his part of the procedure was done, and he was going to be OK. Now all he had to worry about was Ricardo.

Because they weren't blood brothers, the chances of Ricardo's body rejecting the kidney were significant. Plus, clearly the operation Ricardo was undergoing – removing one kidney and replacing it with another, foreign one – was much more involved and carried a far higher risk factor, particularly as Ricky had been so sick to start with. Finally, the news came through that Ricky was out of surgery and had been taken to the Intensive Care unit for observation; all Karl could do was wait.

As the day progressed into evening, the cramps in Karl's muscles grew increasingly uncomfortable and he was given morphine to cope with the pain. Meanwhile, in a different part of the hospital, his old school friend and basketball buddy was starting to stir.

FRIENDS AGAIN...

Even before Ricardo opened his eyes in the intensive care unit, he was aware he felt completely different. His whole body felt lighter, and somehow clearer. As his overjoyed mum and girlfriend bent over him, they were amazed to see the transformation in him. The acne with which his face had been covered in recent years had all but vanished. It was like looking at a different man. As he became more and more awake, Ricardo's feeling of incredulity grew. He'd just come through major surgery, and yet for the first time in his life, he felt healthy.

Later that night, he was wheeled out of intensive care and into a private room next door to Karl, where there was less risk of contamination. Karl was overjoyed to hear that his friend's surgery had been judged a success, but he was well aware, as they all were, that the risk of rejection remained very real.

For the time being, though, the two – heady from the relief of having got the operations over with – were determined to make the most of hospital life. For the two days after surgery, they goofed around, just like old times, ordering food from the hospital menu and playing silly jokes on each other.

Just two days after surgery, Karl was able to leave hospital. After what they'd just been through together, it felt strange to be leaving Ricardo behind, but his friend was in such high spirits, he knew he wouldn't be long behind him. Sure enough, another two days after Karl was discharged, Ricardo too was making his way out through the hospital doors, still marvelling at the change in him since he'd passed through those same doors mere days before.

Just as it seemed everything had gone completely to plan, though, Ricardo suffered a relapse. It was a week after the operation and he was rushed back into the hospital feverish and in pain. For a few agonising days it seemed as if everything might have been for nothing. If Ricardo's body had decided not to accept the new kidney, he would at best facing a lifetime of hospitalisation, being hooked up to a dialysis machine. At worst... well, no one wanted to think about the worst.

Then came the news Karl and Ricky's family had been praying for. Ricardo had pulled through. A few days later, he was once again back home. From then on, recovery was swift and uninterrupted. For the first time in his life, Ricardo was sleeping well and eating well – getting used to a body that functioned as it should.

He and Karl stayed in constant contact, although Karl was anxious right from the start to make sure there was no awkwardness or feeling of obligation getting in the way of their friendship. 'I'm the type of person who, if I want to do something for you, I'll do it and I don't want to hear anything more about it,' he told Ricky soon after the operation. 'So if you want to say "thanks" you say it once and then that's it. OK?'

Ricardo laughingly agreed, knowing that the bond between them was so strong that he didn't need to voice his thanks again and again. His mum on the other hand, was a whole different story. Having nursed Ricardo through a lifetime of hospital visits and sleepless nights, she was having trouble conveying the depth of her gratitude to this man who had emerged from the shadows of the past and changed her son's life.

As Karl returned to the Dominican Republic to take up his medical studies once again, Ricardo had plenty of time on his hands to think about what he wanted to do with the life that had been returned to him. No longer tied to New York's medical system, he was now free to go wherever he chose. It felt dizzyingly liberated.

While in the hospital, he'd made the decision that he'd like to become a doctor himself one day. After all, few people his age were more familiar with the ins and outs of hospital life. From that decision, it was a small but logical step to deciding to specialise in kidneys. Not only did he have a huge amount of specialist knowledge on the subject, he'd also be uniquely placed to empathise with patients – something he knew from experience was vitally important.

Now all that remained was to decide where to study. There was really no contest. By this time, Karl and Ricardo were more than friends: they were brothers. There was no place Ricardo would rather be than with

Karl, sharing in his day-to-day life, hanging out together, studying together.

In September 2008, Ricky flew to the Dominican Republic to begin medical school. It seemed unthinkable that he and Karl shouldn't live together and before long they were inseparable, to the extent that when one was thinking something, the other would express that same thought thing out loud, or Karl would come home to find that Ricky had cooked exactly what he'd been craving to eat. More than brothers even, it was as if Ricardo carrying Karl's kidney, that blood link, made them twins, leading them to finish each other's sentences, think the same thoughts.

For Ricardo who, just a year before, had been facing the prospect of a life on dialysis, it was as if the whole world had opened up to him, full of dazzling possibilities. Karl, in turn, had found a soul mate for life. Both now acknowledge they owe a huge debt of thanks to the website that had brought them back together. 'You hear about all the things that can go wrong with websites like Facebook,' says Karl, now 22. 'But used the right way, they can achieve incredible things.'

CHAPTER NINE
RELATIONSHIP STATUS: SINGLE

Social networking sites boast of helping you stay in touch with people. But what happens when there are people you'd rather not stay in touch with? The following accounts tell of two newly separated women who used a website to tell their friends they were moving on – and paid the ultimate price.

'MY WIFE IS IN THERE – I KILLED HER'

Wayne Forrester tapped the keys on his computer with a mix of excitement, barely repressed fury and self-loathing that had become all too familiar over the last few days.

He knew he shouldn't be doing it. Everyone told him he had to move on with his life. He'd lost count of the number of times he'd heard the phrase 'fresh start' recently. He should be out there, meeting new people, feeling his way towards establishing a different reality, away from the emotional upheaval of the last few years. He knew that. He should be doing everything he could to put some distance between himself and the wife who so clearly wanted him out of her life.

And yet here he was again, preparing to access her Facebook page, like some grubby Peeping Tom.

The idea that the only contact he could get with his own wife, whom he'd been with for the last 15 years, was via a social networking website used by millions, sent another burst of rage shooting through him. How could that be right? He was her husband, the father of her daughters. Why should he be reduced to scouring her updates and comments to friends to find out what she'd been up to, like a stalker going through her rubbish?

In the four days since he'd moved out of the house they'd shared in Croydon, it wasn't the first time Forrester had called up Emma's Facebook page. He couldn't help it. It was like when you had a scab that you knew you should leave alone, but you just couldn't stop picking at. Every time he saw the photo of her on her page, it was as though someone was tying a knot in his gut. That face, at once so familiar and yet already taking on the closed look of a past acquaintance – someone with a separate life, someone with secrets.

As the page loaded, he drummed his fingers impatiently on the table, feeling his anger once again rising. It was she who'd put him in this position, of having to scavenge for information about his own wife like some common busybody. It was she who'd thrown him out and was refusing to have anything more to do with him. And now here he was having to spy on her through her web page, convinced he'd find out there some clues as to what she was *really* getting up to. And more importantly, who with.

Of course, she'd said there was no one else involved, that she'd just had enough of him and his temper. But Wayne wasn't stupid. He knew you didn't break up 15-year relationships just because someone lost control a few times – plenty of men did that. No, there had to be someone else. He was sure of it. He just had to keep checking.

Scanning his eyes over the page, the 34-year-old lorry driver didn't immediately notice anything suspicious. There were no photos of Emma with unidentified men, or flirty comments or indications that she'd been anywhere or was going anywhere out of the ordinary.

But then something caught Wayne Forrester's eye. All of a sudden, a red mist descended over him as he read, and re-read the words with a burning, and growing, sense of outrage. Next to Emma's profile picture, where a few biographical details were listed, showing her date of birth and the area in which she lived, was a heading: 'Relationship status'. Up until now, Emma's had read

'Married to Wayne Forrester'. Now he noticed with a stab of fury that was almost physical, those words had been deleted. Next to Emma Forrester's relationship status there was now just one word: 'Single.'

She had no way of knowing that that one word, typed in a spirit of sudden liberation, would in effect sign her death warrant.

❋   ❋   ❋

New Addington has never enjoyed a very good press. Built mostly after the war in response to Croydon's acute housing shortage, it transmorphed from the original planners' vision of a new garden village, into a series of sprawling estates lacking many of the amenities that many consider necessary for a good quality of life.

True, the addition of a tramline in 2000 helped improve connections and made it easier to travel to Wimbledon and Croydon, but the shopping parade with its dismal selection of pound shops and fast-food outlets does little to enhance the place's rather dismal reputation.

However, across the golf course in Forestdale, the estates are leafier, the cul-de-sacs more cared-for. While there's still the odd bit of litter or graffiti, in place of the abandoned cars and pit bull terriers there are gardens and grass verges and even the odd bridle path. The tramline has helped link residents with outlying towns, removing the necessity to walk or drive through the rougher areas. And on the other side of the development, the Surrey countryside stretches away in a swathe of rolling greenery.

With its useful shops and school, this is the area that those from New Addington aspire to live in. And though there have been a lot of changes in recent years and long-term residents complain that an influx of newcomers and the odd troublemaking family have damaged the sense of community that used to prevail here, they'll still tell you it's not a bad place to live, at least not compared to some.

For Emma Forrester though, Forestdale would never quite seem completely safe. It wasn't the threat from the adolescents in hoods who sometimes roamed the streets, though, or the risk of burglary, which seemed to be rising at an alarming rate. No, Emma Forrester's unease came from a source much closer to home – her husband.

If she were to be honest, life with Wayne had never been an easy ride. Even though they'd been together 15 years – more or less the whole of their adult lives – they'd never had that kind of a peaceful relationship other couples seemed to settle into after a few years. Instead, their relationship had been marked by bitter rows and slamming doors, icy silences and raging tempers. They'd even had periods of separation when Emma had really thought that part of her life was over, only to find herself sucked back into the relationship by the false promises of reconciliation.

There had been times when only the kids had made it bearable, the two girls she doted on beyond anything else. They'd been her driving force since she first became a mother.

While life with Wayne had been full of violent ups and downs, she'd tried her best to keep everything constant for her daughters. She wanted for them the stability and love she'd known herself as a child. So, during the many periods when her husband was out of work, Emma would make sure she worked doubly hard, sometimes doing two jobs at once, to ensure the girls' didn't lose out on anything. Quite regularly Emma's devoted parents, Frances and Robert Rothery, would have to step in financially to bail the family out of debt. The older couple even moved house to be closer to their daughter and granddaughters. For an independent woman, it was hard to accept that she was still having to look to her parents for handouts.

Most recently, Emma been working as a payroll administrator, a job that gave her a steady income and meant she was home early enough to spend time with the girls in the evenings, but still Wayne's contributions were sketchy. 'You deserve so much better than the way he treats you,' her close friends would sometimes say. But Emma was generally more at home in the role of confidante than confider, happier to listen to other people's troubles than to burden them with her own.

Whatever problems she and Wayne had, she tried to deal with them privately.

Towards the end of 2007, tensions increased within the always-volatile marriage, and family and friends of the 34-year-old Emma became worried about her. She always looked so anxious and so preoccupied, even her characteristic warm smile seemed to have lost some of its brightness. Christmas – traditionally a time when repressed domestic resentments rise to the surface – was particularly difficult, and punctuated with arguments that saw Emma's family grouping around her protectively.

No one ever wants to see a couple split up, particularly where children are involved, but many of those who knew Emma Forrester were of the opinion that this was one relationship that had more than run its course. If ever anyone was due a fresh start, they thought, it was her. So it was with a certain degree of relief that people close to Emma heard the news that Wayne had reluctantly moved out of the Forestdale home. It was just before Valentine's Day 2008, and he'd apparently gone to stay with his sister in Paddington – a reassuringly difficult journey across London. At last, they hoped, she and the girls would have a bit of calm.

But any ideas that Forrester's departure might usher in a new period of stability for his estranged wife were dashed almost immediately when he began calling the

TAMMY COHEN

family house, his voice dripping with vitriol and, all too often, alcohol.

'I know you've got someone else,' he'd spit accusingly down the phone. 'I know you're having an affair.' More often than not these calls would end in threats of violence, or even death.

Emma's desperately worried father Robert took to coming to stay in the house, unwilling to leave his daughter alone and unprotected for fear of what his unpredictable son-in-law might do. He and his wife had also been on the receiving end of some of Wayne's ranting phone calls. In particular, he seemed to have got enraged by something Emma had written on a website, although they weren't too sure what it all meant.

On 17 February, Emma's family once again visited her, and were relieved to find her in good spirits, despite the continuing abusive phone calls. 'I've seen what you've done on your Facebook page!' he'd shrieked in some of them. 'Putting yourself down as single and interested in meeting other men. I'm not going to let you get away with it. You're not going to humiliate me like that in front of everyone.'

By this time, though, Emma was becoming more used to her estranged husband's threats and calls. And besides, she was slightly reassured by the distance between her Croydon home and his sister's Paddington flat. Even though it was scarcely more than 10 miles as

194

the crow flies, the journey took you along some of the slowest roads in the capital.

'Don't worry about me,' she told her family. 'I'll be fine.'

And it was true that the smile was once again returning to Emma's face. Maybe not quite as radiant as of old, but certainly a step in the right direction. Wayne surely had to calm down sooner or later. He was bound to realise eventually that threats weren't going to help his cause any.

In a phone call to her sister Liza later that night, Emma once again sounded slightly more optimistic. 'I'm going to bed. I feel really tired. But don't worry about me, I'm going to bolt the front door. I just need to get a good night's sleep.'

Liza had no inkling, as she put the phone down on the sister who'd always been both friend and sibling wrapped up in one, that this was the last time she'd ever hear her voice.

❊   ❊   ❊

More than 10 miles across London, Wayne Forrester had entered a state of sustained and barely suppressed anger. Over the last few days he'd been steadily working through a heap of cocaine, which fuelled both his adrenalin levels and his sense of injustice. This and the copious amount of alcohol also in his system gave him a growing feeling of outrage. How dare she make a fool of him like this? How did she think it felt for him to have to see his wife describe herself as 'single'?

The more he thought about what had happened, the greater his rage became. He hadn't wanted to leave the marital home – as far as he was concerned, he'd been forced to leave. And now it was all making sense. She wanted to get someone else in his place. Well, she'd soon see she couldn't play around with people's emotions like that. She'd soon see she'd made a huge mistake. She wasn't going get away with it. She was going to pay.

While Emma Forrester was locking her doors against the threat of intrusion, and tiptoeing past her 6-year-old's bedroom, Wayne was starting to make plans. His wife was going to regret making him leave his own home and more specifically she was going to regret deleting him from her web page, as easily as if she was deleting him from her life.

Driving across London a short while later, he took care not to appear under the influence of anything. The last thing he wanted was to be pulled up by the police. As a HGV driver, he couldn't afford to risk any points on his licence. And then there was the little matter of the objects he'd brought along with him on the journey. How on earth would he explain to police why he was driving through the capital with a sharp knife and a meat cleaver next to him in the car?

✳   ✳   ✳

At 6.30am on 18 February 2008, the normally peaceful early morning atmosphere in Forestdale was shattered by an ear-splitting crack. Moments later, the sound of a woman's high pitched screaming filled the air around 265 Markfield, a residential cul-de-sac off Courtwood Lane.

'Police, please. It's urgent.'

But even as the neighbours were whispering nervously into their cordless phones, curtains twitching at the window, inside number 265 it was all over. The horrific screams, which would linger on in the memories of all those who heard them, had now stopped, and instead an eerie silence hung over the house, a tense, pulsing muscle-bound silence, as when someone is lying completely still in bed, but wide awake on soundless alert.

And then, as the first police sirens sounded in the distance, the caved-in front door opened, and Wayne Forrester appeared, swaggering in the pre-dawn semi-darkness of that February early morning, clutching a carton of fruit juice in his hand.

He watched calmly as the police car screeched to a halt outside the house. Then he held out his hands in front of him as if waiting to be cuffed. There was a collective intake of breath as the onlookers took in the state of Forrester's hands.

'Isn't that...?' the neighbours gasped to one another. 'Please let it not be...'

But there could be no mistaking it. Even in the

grainy early morning light, there was no getting away from the fact that Wayne Forrester's hands were covered with blood.

And all of a sudden they became aware of another sound – a child's voice coming from inside the house. 'Help me. Help me.'

Police officers shot inside and up the stairs, emerging some time later, ashen faced and carrying something large, but clearly fragile, wrapped up carefully in a duvet.

This was the child who would never officially be identified (the whereabouts of the two Forrester girls would never be made public), the child who had witnessed something that morning that no one should ever have to see, and had herself dialled 999 earlier on, her high-pitched, trembling voice almost drowned out by the chilling screams in the background.

For inside that neat family home, where once a loving mother had, bleary-eyed, prepared packed lunches on bleak, half-lit winter mornings, or sat on the edge of a bed to stroke a feverish child's clammy forehead, Emma Forrester now lay still in the hallway, gazing glassily at the ceiling with unseeing eyes. Blood, deep red and shockingly thick, pooled around her from an ugly, gaping wound in her neck. There were also cuts on her head, stomach, arms and hands, and clumps of hair where she'd been dragged from her bedroom. Two banister rods were broken, splinters of wood embedded in the carpet like needles. Next to her body was a large kitchen knife, blood cloying stickily around the blade. In another room was a crimson-stained meat cleaver.

Here was a woman who had fought for her life. Here was a mother who had battled to her last breath for the chance to see her daughters grow up, watch them get married, help them look after their own babies in time.

From the minute she'd woken up to everyone's worst nightmare – a man leaning over the bed, meat cleaver in one hand, kitchen knife in the other, his breath fetid with stale alcohol, his eyes devoid of humanity or compassion, almost of recognition – she'd fought back, clawing at him with resisting hands as he raised the cleaver over his head again and again...

Outside the still-echoing house, Wayne Forrester held his bloodied hands out to police. 'Who called you?' he asked conversationally, eyeing the coating of blood as calmly as if it were a smattering of red paint. Then he added: 'My wife is in there. I killed her.' The words, so matter-of-factly spoken, seemed to hang in the eerie first light long after the tail-lights of the police car taking Forrester from the scene had disappeared around the corner of the cul-de-sac.

❉   ❉   ❉

On 17 October 2008, eight months after Wayne Forrester made his murderous journey across London to kill his wife, an Old Bailey judge sentenced him to life imprisonment with a recommendation that he spend at least 14 years behind bars.

At a previous hearing, Forrester had admitted murdering Emma but had claimed he'd been provoked into acting the way he did. 'Emma and I had just split up. She forced me out of the family home and posted messages on the Internet website telling everybody she had left me and was interested in meeting other men,' he wrote in a prepared statement to police. 'I loved Emma and felt totally devastated and humiliated about what she had done to me.'

Forrester went on to claim that he had entered a kind of altered state when carrying out the murder, in which he'd been outside his own body, looking on as if watching a particularly violent horror film. 'The whole incident seemed a blur,' he claimed. 'I felt as if I was watching somebody else attacking Emma.'

But for Emma's bereft family, left behind to pick up the pieces of a young life prematurely and violently torn from its roots, Wayne Forrester's justifications, and his oft-repeated protestations of remorse, mean nothing. 'She was my friend and I miss her dreadfully,' Emma's grieving sister Liza wrote in an emotional impact statement read to the court. 'I wasn't there to help her and I share my parents' feelings of guilt for this... Life will never be the same for any of us again... One action has exploded like a bomb in our family.'

'CURRENTLY SPLITTING UP FROM MY HUSBAND'

'We're splitting up.'

If Tracey Grinhaff had told her friends she was moving to Mars, she couldn't have shocked them more than she did with the bombshell that her marriage was over. No one had seen it coming.

Tracey and Gary had been together 26 years. They'd known each other since school days. They'd lived in their comfortable semi in Wombwell, South Yorkshire, for nearly two decades and had two daughters they both adored beyond measure. They were the sort of couple you just knew would be together forever. They even finished each other's sentences. Surely this would turn out to be some momentary blip, some kind of early mid-life crisis?

But Tracey, normally so affable, so loath to cause offence or upset, was adamant. Things hadn't been right for a while now. She was 42 years old – if she didn't make the break now, when would she get the courage to do it? Would she spend the rest of her life regretting the chance she didn't take? She and Gary were still young enough to make new lives for themselves with new partners who maybe were better suited to the people they were now, rather than the people they'd been 26 years ago. She knew it was going to be tough for the next few months, particularly for the girls, but it would work out for the best in the end, she was sure. She just wished she could convince Gary of that.

Tracey's friends were taken aback, but nevertheless they rallied around her. Tracey had a reputation for being a warm-hearted, generous person who'd go that little bit extra to help out a friend. They weren't about to abandon her now. And who cared if there were rumours that the attractive blonde mum-of-two had been seeing somebody else? People would always point the finger in situations like this, trying to find a neat little label to pin onto the nebulous, indefinable mess that most marriage break-ups were.

No, if Tracey wanted, even needed, to make a fresh start for whatever reason, she had plenty of support. And when she changed her Facebook profile so that it read 'Currently splitting up from my husband', many of her friends applauded her honesty. There was no point, was there, in hiding from the truth? It was going to come out some time, so why not be upfront about it? Everyone would find out soon enough.

But there was one person who didn't appreciate Tracey Grinhaff's candour, written in black and white on her social networking page for the world to read. There was one person who didn't think it a positive thing for Tracey to announce the end of a 26-year relationship in a brief sentence on a semi-public website.

That person was Gary Grinhaff, Tracey's husband for the last 16 years.

Every time he looked at the photo of a sun-bleached Tracey, wearing a pink dress and clasping the couple's youngest daughter Niamh, which graced Tracey's Facebook page, Gary was reminded all over again of everything he'd lost, and everything he still stood to lose. In his emotionally overwrought and sleep-deprived brain, it almost felt like she was publicly taunting him.

There were times when the 44-year-old electrical engineer just didn't know whether he could physically bear it. His life, which up to now had been so steady, so charmed almost – his beautiful wife, his loving girls – had been brutally churned and ploughed up so that it now bore no resemblance to the orderly, satisfying existence he'd had before. How did one cope with that? Gary wondered miserably. How did one start again alone after quarter of a century with the same woman? How did one start a new life when one was still in mourning for the old one?

At night the questions went round and round Gary Grinhaff's head. Ever since he'd discovered some weeks before that his wife, Tracey was having an affair with a married family friend, his ordered, enviable life had been plunged into turmoil.

At an April crisis meeting between the Grinhaffs and the other couple involved, Tracey and her lover had agreed to stop seeing each other. But for Gary the flames of suspicion, once ignited, proved impossible to put out.

He started spying obsessively on his wife, even bugging his own home phone and planting a tracking device on her Nissan 4-wheel drive. He'd promised Tracey he'd spend more time with the family in an effort at reconciliation, but instead he increasingly locked himself away, obsessively checking up on his wife through his surveillance equipment.

While he still managed to present an image to the outside world of a man just about holding it together, internally Gary Grinhaff was a mess. Images of his wife with another man crept unbidden into his dreams, making it impossible for him to sleep and loosening his grip on reality.

He bought an old Ford Escort for £350 which he parked on a nearby housing estate. Wearing a variety of disguises, he'd sink down behind the steering wheel and follow Tracey as she pulled out away from their house, keeping just far enough away for her not to get unduly alarmed.

Deep down, in the rational part of his brain he knew he shouldn't be doing all this, but it was as though something had taken him over and the thoughts that most tortured him were the very ones he could least keep at bay. Gary Grinhaff's family was at the very centre of his life, and now it was as if someone had kicked that centre away, sending him spinning into freefall, all familiar reference points lost.

When he saw, a short while after the four-way crisis meeting, that Tracey had updated her Facebook page to include that fateful statement, 'currently splitting up with my husband', it just increased his sense of being alienated from all that was reassuring and comfortable in his life. At night he agonised on it sleeplessly. How did anyone live through this level of heartbreak, this level of loss? How did anyone endure it?

And yet during the daytime, he clung to the façade that nothing was wrong. Visiting his father, Arthur, at the end of April 2008, he gave no indication that anything was amiss either with his marriage or with his state of mind. 'Oh yes, the family's fine Dad,' he reassured him in answer to the older man's usual polite concern.

Neighbours in Aldham Crescent, where the Grinhaffs were such familiar faces, saw nothing unusual about the quiet, self-contained family man. To all intents and purposes, he was the same solid dependable Gary he always had been. And yet inside his head, Gary Grinhaff was far from fine. His life was unravelling in front of his eyes and all he could do was watch.

❋ ❋ ❋

Six o'clock in the morning.

Aldham Crescent doesn't usually show much signs of

life at this time in the morning – just the occasional neon flash of the paper boy's bag in the faint early light. But on 2 May 2008, all that changed. Suddenly the groggy peace of the normally placid suburban street was disturbed by the sound of the front door of number 9 opening and the echoing footsteps of children running. Seconds later, they were knocking frantically on a neighbour's door, the hollow thuds resonating in the still post-dawn air. Then voices raised in urgency and the passing over of a note.

After that, everything was different.

In place of the usual morning routine of curtains opening first in upstairs, then downstairs windows, and goodbyes called over shoulders as children trudge off to school, laden bags pulling on their backs, Aldham Crescent became a hotbed of feverish activity. Police cars drew up outside number 9 and officers swept through the empty house, before opening the back door and searching the outbuildings. Then a shout went up, and all of a sudden there were more police cars, and now there was also police tape going up around the house, fencing in whatever secrets it was keeping. The entrance to the road was also taped up. When a Meals-on-Wheels van tried to enter, the driver was forced to park and carry the food through on foot.

The residents, finding themselves suddenly virtual prisoners in their own homes, whispered among themselves. Rumours were circulating that the

Grinhaff girls – Niamh, 3, and Chloe, 13 – had turned up at a neighbour's house with a note saying something 'bad' had happened to their parents. Impossibly, Tracey's body had been found in a back shed. She'd been murdered.

Murdered. The word jarred in the peaceful suburban surroundings, discordant and obscene. Murders didn't happen in places like Wombwell. They happened on run-down inner-city streets, or lawless sink estates. And the victims were drug dealers or gang members. They weren't middle-aged housewives who took their toddlers to mother-and-baby groups and baked cakes for the school cake sale.

What had gone on behind the ordinary brown-brick façade of number 9, with its friendly arched doorway and neat trellis, where Tracey had been trying to encourage a climbing plant to grow? How had a family that had seemed so perfect from the outside become so desperately unstuck? And, most pressing of all, where on earth was Gary?

The answer came all too soon.

Just an hour after the shocking discovery in Aldham Crescent, police swooped on Wombwell Woods, a local beauty spot a mile from Aldham Crescent, where a car had been spotted among the trees. There they found Gary Grinhaff, also dead.

The rest of that day passed in a blur of sirens and

questions for the residents of Aldham Crescent. Had they seen anything unusual? Had the Grinhaffs been acting out of character?

No one seemed to know what had happened. There were reports that a man had been arrested, but later released without charge. There were rumours – about an affair, a love triangle, that note the girls had been carrying.

As news spread of the double tragedy, flowers were laid outside the house where the popular mother-of-two had been killed. 'Words can't express…' the cards read, 'So shocked to hear…' How could anyone begin to make sense of a thing like this? Murder lived in New York, London, Manchester. It didn't live in a suburban semi in Wombwell.

The world, it seemed, had gone mad and the more details emerged, the madder the world seemed. On May 1st, Gary had finished an early shift at 2pm and returned home to spend the evening with his family. During the past weeks he'd been sleeping in elder daughter Chloe's room, while she shared with her mum, but on this night he asked Chloe to return to her own bed so he could spend the night with his wife.

The following morning, Chloe was awoken by the sound of her little sister, Niamh, crying. Staggering out of bed, she found the three-year-old standing on the landing sobbing that she couldn't find Mummy or Daddy. With a growing feeling of unease, the older girl popped her head around the door of her parents' bedroom and saw the empty bed uncovered, with a pile of towels on the floor next to it.

Going downstairs to fetch her sister a glass of milk, Chloe's heart was hammering. Where would her parents be at this time in the morning? It was completely out of character for them to leave them alone. Venturing fearfully into the kitchen, Chloe's attention was caught by a note pinned to the extractor hood of the oven. She recognised her father's writing immediately.

Finally, here would be the explanation she'd been hoping for. But instead of setting her mind at rest, the note just increased Chloe's fears one hundred fold. 'Go to the neighbours', the terrified girl was instructed. 'Tell them something bad has happened.'

When police arrived at Aldham Crescent, they searched the house. Pulling aside the towels from the floor of the master bedroom, they were aghast to find they hid bloodstains that pooled dark and ugly on the carpet. Clearly someone had wanted to make sure the children didn't see what lay underneath. From that second there was a heightened sense of foreboding that spread through the atmosphere of the house, like a tangible presence. Everyone's worst fears were confirmed when, moments later, Tracey's pyjama-clad body was found in the garage, partially wrapped in a duvet, her blonde hair matted with blood.

Less than an hour later, while the engines of the police cars on the road outside the Granhaff's home were still warm, the local police station received an anxious call from a member of the public who thought they'd seen someone lying outside a car in nearby woods. The body turned out to be Gary. He also had deep wounds – this time to his arms and legs, only his were self inflicted. Incredible though it would appear to all who knew them, this caring, devoted husband and father had murdered his wife and then killed himself, orphaning his own beloved daughters in the process. It was inconceivable.

Just how inconceivable was revealed in the inquest into the deaths, on 9 February 2009. After killing Tracey with a heavy, blunt instrument, which was never found, a desperate Gary had driven out to woodland half a mile from his home. There he had carefully laid out two notes in the Ford Escort – one to Chloe and one to the other couple involved in the love triangle. 'This cannot go on, this is my only way out,' he'd written.

Afterwards, he'd attempted to kill himself in a number of ways – first by pumping the car with poisonous fumes from the exhaust, then by trying to roll the car on top of himself. Finally, in desperation, he'd seized a cordless drill from the car, carried it outside and started drilling holes into his arms and legs. A post mortem showed he died from haemorrhage and shock caused by the gaping wounds. A shockingly violent end for someone remembered almost universally by those who knew him as the gentlest of men.

❋   ❋   ❋

Gary Grinhaff and Wayne Forrester were two men who, for very different reasons, found the ending of their marriages impossible to accept. Of course, both would still have struggled to accept their break-ups even if they hadn't been able to track their estranged wives' movements via a social networking site. But in both cases, seeing their former partners publicly acknowledging the relationship was over on a website that could be accessed by family and friends, was one of the factors that contributed to them losing control in the most catastrophic and tragic way.

Without doubt, social networking sites are a fantastic way of keeping those around us updated with what's happening in our lives. Just remember, though: there are some people you might prefer to keep in the dark.

CHAPTER TEN
'I KNEW YOU FIRST'

'**Y**ou'll never guess who just sent me an email through Friends Reunited!'

The unmistakeable high-pitched voice of her best friend, Rosie, came screeching long-distance down the phone line.

Anna, who'd been woken up by the ringing of the phone, struggled blearily to come up with a suitable response. But she wasn't quick enough for Rosie.

'Chris Robinson!' she squealed impatiently, before exploding into giggles.

Now Anna really was properly awake. Chris Robinson. Immediately she was transported back across three decades to the tarmac playground of her suburban London primary school. She remembered the unflattering bottle-green skirt she'd had to wear and the blue-and-yellow tie she'd knotted, as they all had, rakishly wide. And she remembered, almost as if it were just the other day a small boy with thick, brown hair and a long, thin face standing with his friends by the football goals, shooting her the occasional smile across the playground when no one was looking.

'He was asking for your email address,' Rosie was saying breathlessly.

'You didn't give it to him, did you?'

Rosie laughed. 'What do you take me for? 'Course I did!'

Anna groaned, but inside there was a part of her that was quite excited. Chris Robinson had been her first boyfriend. He'd been around long before life got so complicated with mortgages and moves abroad and partners who didn't appreciate you. Wouldn't it be a laugh to hear from him again?

As if reading her mind – which, after all these years she probably could – Rosie chimed in: 'Oh it's only a bit of fun, Anna. After all, you're over there in Portugal and he's over here. It's not as if Dom has got anything to worry about.'

Anna shot a glance over at her still-sleeping boyfriend, snoring softly, his arms thrown up over his head. Chance would be a fine thing. Dom was so uninterested in her life these days he probably wouldn't care less if Chris Robinson turned up on their doorstep declaring undying love. 'I guess there's no harm in it,' she conceded.

Little could Anna have known that, just weeks after that phone call in May 2003, she'd be fighting to save the relationship she'd so casually taken for granted. Or that Chris Robinson, her tousle-haired, grubby-faced childhood Romeo, would turn out to be anything but harmless.

❋   ❋   ❋

Romantic relationships at the age of ten have little in common with those that come later in life. For a start, you don't actually have to talk with the object of your affection. In fact, you don't really have to have that much affection for them either. Generally, you get your friend to ask them out on your behalf, then you maybe carry their bag home, or let your bag be carried home a couple of times. And then the same friend who asked you out in the first place sidles over to tell you you're chucked. And that's that.

No wonder Anna Collins had always looked back on her playground romance with Chris Robinson with a certain amount of nostalgia. 'Pathetic though our relationship undoubtedly was, he was my first-ever boyfriend,' she was fond of telling people. In the way of these things, the romance was over within weeks, after Anna decided Chris was a poor substitute for her real love – Donny Osmond.

After Chris went off to another school at the age of 12 the two never saw each other again. So Anna was rather thrilled when, the very day of Rosie's call, an email from Chris plopped into her inbox, telling her how he'd always thought of her fondly over the years and how, even aged ten, she'd always managed to make him laugh.

It so happened that Chris' email came at a particularly unsettled time in Anna's life. She'd moved to Portugal two years before with Dom, her boyfriend of ten years, and she was still unsure whether she'd made the right decision. An only child, she missed her family back in Brentwood terribly and found herself forgetting all about the things that had driven her mad about England – the dark winter afternoons, the crowded trains. Instead, looking back through the rose-tinted glasses of a voluntary exile, she allowed her nostalgia free reign, focusing on long summer evenings sitting outside country pubs and happy get-togethers with good friends. And more and more, she remembered schooldays, where everything was easy and there were no responsibilities or tough decisions.

It didn't help that she and Dom were going through a particularly difficult patch in their relationship. They'd been together such a long time that each had stopped making much of an effort with the other. Anna couldn't remember the last time Dom had paid her a compliment or surprised her with a night out or a bunch of flowers. It hadn't seemed to bother her before, but she was 34 years old and couldn't help wondering whether this was really the person she wanted to be with as she prepared for the lead-up to 40. Was she ready to settle for this easy but unchallenging relationship, where both of them plodded along side by side like a couple of docile shire ponies? Was she really prepared to sacrifice passion for companionship?

Her discontent had prompted her to book a solo holiday back to the UK, in July of that year. She was planning to stay with her parents back in Brentwood for the first week, before joining them in a rented cottage in Devon. It would give her a chance to get a bit of perspective on her life, she'd decided.

So it would be fair to say Anna was at a bit of a crossroads when Chris' email turned up, nudging open a door to the past that she'd long thought closed. She spent a long time labouring over a reply that was witty and at the same time ever so slightly flirtatious. As she hit 'send', she thought about how easy it would be to reinvent yourself totally – moulding yourself into the person you wished you were, rather than the person you really are. Here she was taking such pains to be amusing and bubbly, yet when was the last time she'd taken that kind of trouble for Dom?

As she'd been secretly hoping, her email was closely

followed by another message from Chris, matching her flirtatious tone and making her snort with laughter as he reminded her of incidents from the long-distant past that she'd buried deep in her memory. How refreshing it was to be able to exchange light-hearted banter without having to bother about any boring, mundane practicalities. How liberating it felt to be free to be her brightest, most sparkling self, unencumbered by lingering resentment over housework or who'd forgotten to pay the phone bill.

Over the following few days, the email correspondence gathered momentum and Anna found herself giving more and more thought to her erstwhile beau. Everything he said seemed so funny and clever. And his job in TV was so much more glamorous than anyone else she knew. Certainly, Dom's job as an electrician didn't seem nearly as exciting. Chris was married with a young daughter, but it was obvious to Anna that the relationship wasn't very happy. He'd told her he regretted rushing into marriage and he'd also hinted at feeling trapped. His wife had given up work when their child was born and had never gone back with the result, he complained, that they seemed to have less and less to talk about.

Anna couldn't help imagining what it would be like to be married to Chris. They'd both come home from work in the evening full of anecdotes and interesting snippets from their days. She knew he lived in a house in a very nice part of London and she imagined how they'd nip out to an intimate restaurant round the corner, or off to catch a movie in one of the nearby art-house cinemas. It all seemed so sophisticated compared to the life she and Dom were leading in Portugal. Sure, Lisbon was beautiful and they got to explore amazing scenery at the weekends, but it was a little on the provincial side compared to the glamour and buzz of metropolitan London, which she missed so much.

Gradually, the emails between Anna and Chris increased both in volume and intimacy. Anna confided that she felt she'd reached a stalemate in her relationship with Dom, while Chris revealed more of his deep-seated unhappiness in his marriage. 'If it wasn't for my daughter, Lizzy, I'd be long gone,' he told her.

But most of the time, their emails were perfectly crafted to be clever and humorous. Anna found herself keeping an eye on newspaper headlines that she could fashion into amusing conversation pieces or witty one-liners. It made such a change from the exchanges she had with Dom which, these days, seemed to hinge more on what they needed from the supermarket than any desire to keep one another entertained.

As the day of her flight back to the UK approached, the correspondence between Dom and Anna took on a greater urgency. They'd already arranged a sort of mini reunion with other old classmates, including Rosie, and the knowledge that they were actually going to meet in person turned what had been low-level flirting into a full-blown cyber affair.

Each admitted how much they were looking forward to seeing the other. Each fantasised privately of being swept off their feet and disappearing off into the sunset hand in hand, as in all good movies. Anna was flattered to learn how Chris had always remembered her for her beautiful eyes and her uncompromising honesty. In turn, she recalled her memories of how he used to walk her home, carrying her bag, and how subsequent 'boyfriends' had never seemed to make her laugh quite so much.

They talked a lot about the reunion and how nerve-racking it was going to be. Which led, naturally, to a suggestion that they might meet up beforehand, just the two of them, so that it wouldn't seem so scary. 'If we run out of things to say, we can always play kiss chase, like the old days,' Chris suggested.

Funnily enough, the idea of swapping recent photos was never mentioned. Anna did point out that she could turn out to be 28 stone, instead of the goddess she clearly was. But, they agreed, they could wait to see one another in the flesh.

'Will you still be carrying your satchel?' Anna joked, but secretly she imagined him grown up into a tall, handsome figure with a brooding, slightly melancholy face. She let slip accidentally on purpose that Dom was away on business, knowing that Chris would ask if he could call her, which he did. The two of them started having long, intimate phone chats in which they talked about anything and everything, sparking off one another so the conversation seemed energised and electric.

'For the first time in years, this is all about *me*,' Anna tried to explain to a highly amused Rosie. 'It's not about work or family or mortgages or gas bills, it's just about me. Someone is actually interested in me.'

The emails grew even more frequent. Despite telling herself it was all still perfectly harmless – and nothing had really happened – Anna still took the trouble to create a Hotmail account separate from her usual email address in which she stored Chris' emails, often reading and re-reading them again and again.

By the time Anna flew back to the UK, she was a nervous wreck. Although she'd kept telling herself she didn't need to feel guilty, because after all it was just a bit of light-hearted cyber flirtation, she couldn't help feeling choked with guilt when Dom drove her to the airport and gave her a huge cuddle. 'I know things have been a bit difficult lately,' he said, surprising her with his perceptiveness. 'But I am really going to miss you.'

It's all right, she told herself on the long flight back. Nothing has happened and nothing is going to happen.

It was all just a bit of fun that got out of hand. But when her mobile rang before she'd even had a chance to get out of Luton, she couldn't deny the thrill that passed through her as Chris' name popped up on the screen (or rather 'Christina', the pseudonym she'd given him in case Dom should get hold of it). Even though they'd been talking on the phone for days now, there was a new sense of illicit pleasure that came from knowing they were sharing the same soil for the first time.

'Good to have you home,' Chris told her, and she felt a sudden jolt at the last word. Home? Surely home should be with Dom? So how come it felt like he was right?

They'd arranged to meet on the Thursday evening, the night before the main reunion on Friday. All of that Thursday, Anna felt by turns queasy and excited, and even though she'd only brought a limited selection of clothes with her, she still tried on every possible permutation before settling on a pair of new jeans, with a dressy white top that showed her Portuguese suntan off to perfection.

She and Dom had arranged to meet on a street corner near both their childhood homes. It was chosen both for its proximity to the pub they intended to go to, but also because it was where, in the long distant past, they used to go their separate ways after walking home from school together.

As she approached the designated meeting spot, Anna could feel her nervousness growing by the second. Rounding the bend, she saw a figure up ahead and had to restrain herself from turning and running back home, so overwhelmed was she with sudden panic. Forcing herself to continue moving forwards, she was struck by two thoughts as the waiting figure grew closer: 1) he was shorter than she was and 2) she didn't know why she'd imagined he'd have transformed into an Adonis – he looked exactly the same as he had at 12, but with slightly less hair.

Trying to disguise the disappointment she felt sure must show in her face, Anna greeted Chris with a smile and a clumsy hug before they set off side by side to the pub. As they walked, they chatted about how weird it all was, and how nervous they'd both been. Before long, Anna found she'd stopped thinking about what he looked like and was just enjoying talking to him, their conversation equally sparkling in real life as it had been long-distance. But there was no doubting it, the chemistry she'd been secretly expecting was missing – on her side, at least.

When the barman called last orders, Anna was shocked at how quickly the time had passed, and they reluctantly put their jackets back on and stepped back out into the spring night. Approaching 'their' corner, she began to get butterflies in her stomach. She knew Chris was going to kiss her and, despite her initial reservations, she knew she wasn't going to say no. She'd been building up to this moment for the last few weeks and wasn't about to let a few inches of height or a slightly receding hairline stand in the way of fulfilling her fantasies. Soon she'd be going back to Dom and the boring sameness of their life together. Surely she was entitled to a few harmless moments of fairy tale?

'It's just like a holiday romance,' she giggled down her mobile to Rosie as she walked the short distance home after leaving Chris.

But later on, when she received a text from him saying how much he was looking forward to seeing her at the reunion the next night, she wasn't so sure. 'I think I could fall in love with you,' he'd written. Surely he wasn't attaching any importance to what they both must know was a brief holiday flirtation?

Still, by the following night, she'd managed to dismiss that as the product of a little too much red wine in the pub. Nothing in their correspondence to date had alluded even vaguely to a future together, and though she had got a bit carried away with fantasies of being swept off her feet and whisked off into a glamorous new life, now she'd met Chris again, she realised it wasn't going to happen. Even if he'd been the tall, dark, handsome figure of her imagination, she knew deep down she wouldn't have given up Dom and all the history they had together.

But that didn't mean she couldn't have a bit of fun now she was here. Once she got back to Portugal, it'd be back to the same old same old. This was her chance for a little bit of adventure. And really, at the end of the day, it was only flirting, nothing serious. Of course, that didn't stop her splashing out over £50 on a new dress the next afternoon, but she told herself it was for the old classmates she'd be meeting up with at the reunion, not for Chris.

The evening was a huge success. There were about 25 people there, many of whom hadn't seen each other in decades, and the laughter was soon flowing as fast as the drinks as they recalled teachers and incidents long buried in the hazy mists of time. But all the time she was talking to other people, Anna was aware of Chris' eyes following her around the room. It was quite flattering, but at the same time she couldn't help feeling a little uneasy. There was something so intense about his gaze, she was sure the others must be able to sense something. Sure enough, Rosie came up to her.

'Grab your coat, you've pulled!' she joked. 'He can't take his eyes off you.'

At the end of the night, Chris materialised by her side, clearly ready to walk her home and for the first time Anna was quite relieved she was going on holiday with her parents the next day. He was just as witty and amusing as ever, but she couldn't shake off a low-level anxiety that perhaps he was imagining more to it than there was.

Sure enough, after they stopped on 'their' corner, he said: 'I've arranged to be away on a job in Bristol for a couple of days next week. Why don't you come back from holiday early and join me? We've been given a second chance at happiness here, both of us. Let's not blow it.'

He was gazing at her intently as he spoke, his brown eyes boring into hers. Just a day or two ago, Anna would have been thrown into a dilemma by his proposition, knowing deep down she couldn't go through with it, but still deeply tempted, and unable to resist fantasising about how it might have been. But suddenly she realised there had been a shift. She no longer felt as though Chris was holding the door open on a whole world of adventure that been closed off to her by her safe, boring life with Dom. Instead, she saw him for what he was – a short, average-looking, nearly middle-aged man who felt trapped and was looking for somebody, anybody, to come and rescue him.

Knowing she was going off on holiday the next day and wouldn't see him again, she took the easy option and didn't say outright what was going through her mind, instead telling him she'd see what she could do but couldn't really see how it would be possible. 'But it's been lovely seeing you again,' she told him brightly, already edging slightly away. 'I'll always remember these few days.'

Before she'd even got to the front door, Chris had texted her to make sure she was home. She replied as briefly as possible and then, guiltily, turned off her phone. That night, before she went to sleep, she sent a long email to Dom, telling him she was missing him, and couldn't wait to get back. She could just picture the baffled expression on his familiar face as he read it – they weren't a couple given to elaborate displays of affection. Coming so close to doing something stupid with Chris just brought home to her how special her relationship with Dom was, and how much she wanted to make it work.

In the car on the way to Devon the next morning, Anna felt lighter with each passing mile, as if she were unburdening herself gradually. How stupid she'd been, she scolded herself, and what a good thing she'd come to her senses before anything happened. A couple of times, her phone buzzed with another message from 'Christina', but she didn't open them. She'd had a quick look at her emails early in the morning before leaving, and seen he'd sent her a long one detailing his plans for them to get together in Bristol, including a description of the hotel he'd booked – a trendy boutique place even Anna had heard of. She couldn't bear the guilt of reading his text messages elaborating on the plan she alone knew was a pipedream.

It was getting on for midday when her phone rang. Checking the caller display she realised it was Dom and answered with a warm, 'Hi, babe.' But the response she got was anything but friendly. 'I've had a most fascinating morning,' he told her, his voice eerily expressionless. 'I've just been reading your heart-warming emails.'

Anna had heard the expression 'blood running cold' but until this moment, she'd never really comprehended exactly what it meant. Yelling at her dad to pull over, she begged Dom to stay on the line while she climbed out of the car and onto the hard shoulder of the motorway. 'It was just a bit of harmless flirtation,' she told him. 'Nothing happened. We met up at the reunion, and went our separate ways.'

Dom wasn't buying it. 'Then you won't mind giving me the password of the secret Hotmail email account you opened,' he said icily.

Anna was stunned. 'But how did you…?'

'It wasn't exactly hard to find a record of it in your "history",' Dom retorted. 'After all, you seemed to log on to it every minute of the day. 'If you want there to be any future between us, you have to give me that password. Now.'

In vain did Anna try reasoning with him, or feigning amnesia. The ultimatum was clear. Either she told him her password here and now, or they were finished.

Miserably, Anna recounted her password and listened to the click as Dom immediately hung up on her.

As the car continued on towards Devon, she sat mutely in the back, refusing to answer her parents' increasingly concerned questions, just going over and over in her head what Dom was going to find in that email account. All those messages about how he took her for granted and didn't appreciate her, all those flirty question-and-answer sessions. Then, she sat upright as she remembered the email she'd barely glanced at this morning with its detailed description of the hotel Chris had booked for them, and exactly how she could travel down there.

'Stop the car again!' she screeched to her father.

Once again, he reluctantly pulled over onto the hard shoulder, while Anna frantically dialled both the landline and Dom's mobile number. No answer. 'It's not what you think,' she yelled into the answerphone, second time round. 'I never intended to go through with it.'

All through the remainder of the journey, she tried in vain to get through to Dom. At the cottage, which had no phone reception, she sat miserably curled up in an armchair, immune to the charms of the Aga kitchen or the beautiful sea view.

Every hour she'd borrow her dad's car and drive five minutes to the nearest village, where she'd attempt to call Dom from the phone box, piles of coins at the ready. Even though it was the middle of the night there, she knew he wouldn't be sleeping. But no answer.

Finally, at around 11pm he picked up.

'I'm so sorry,' she sobbed, dissolving into tears the minute she heard his familiar voice. 'I was just feeling so old and ugly and over-the-hill and I was flattered to have someone taking an interest in me. I should never have encouraged him, but I never meant to go through with it. I love you so much. Please believe me.'

Dom listened impassively, but when he spoke she could hear the hurt in his voice. 'Tell me *exactly* what happened, from start to finish,' he told her. 'I'm not sure how I feel about you any more. But you tell me any more lies and it's completely over.'

So Anna painfully reconstructed the history of her reunion with Chris Robinson, leaving nothing out. Not even the kisses at the corner. When she'd finished, she felt drained, and clearly so did Dom. 'I need to go away and think about everything,' he told her woodenly. 'I suggest you do the same.' He told her to call in a couple of days' time, when they'd both had a chance to digest everything that had happened, and work out what they wanted to happen now.

It was the longest two days Anna had ever known. While her parents spent their time poring over local maps and discovering hidden beaches and picturesque villages, Anna stayed in the house, gazing at the photo of Dom she carried in her handbag and weeping as all the memories of things they'd done together came flooding back to her.

How could she have risked everything for what she could see now had been a mere ego boost? How could she even have compared Chris, with his London pretensions that barely disguised his emotional neediness, with kind, funny, well-balanced Dom? As the designated time for the phone call grew closer, the knot in her insides was pulled tighter and tighter. What would Dom have to say? The thought of him telling her it was over was so unbearable, and yet she kept thinking back to the hurt in his voice, and all those terrible things she'd said in her emails.

Dialling the number from the phone box, she could see her jacket moving where her heart was hammering against her chest. Her whole life as she knew it hung on this one phone call. When Dom answered the phone, she could hardly raise her voice above a whisper. 'I'm so sorry,' she told him, before he'd even had a chance to speak. 'I want to make it work. I'll do anything.'

There followed a silence, which seemed to stretch on endlessly ahead, interminable as a foggy day. Then, just when Anna could bear it no longer, Dom finally spoke. 'You're right. I was taking you for granted,' he said gruffly in what was obviously a rehearsed speech. 'I

TAMMY COHEN

always loved you, but I got complacent and I guess I stopped showing you.

'You'll never know how much this has hurt me. But I know I've got to take some of the blame, so I'm willing to give us another chance. If you are.'

Now Anna really couldn't speak. There was a lump in her throat the size of an orange and she could hardly see the phone dial in front of her for the tears blurring her vision. 'Yes,' was all she could manage. 'Yes, yes, yes.'

Over the next few days, Anna worked her way through towers of pound coins talking to Dom over the phone about what had gone wrong, and what they could do to make sure it didn't happen again. Making a special journey to an Internet café, she sent a message to Chris telling him that though it had been nice to see him again, she loved Dom and was going home to make a go of things with him. She knew Dom would read the message, so she made sure to keep it businesslike and unequivocal. Hitting 'send', she felt relief course through her as if she were finally slamming closed the door on what had been a particularly painful episode in her life.

The following day, Anna and her parents drove back to London, with Anna in a considerably more buoyant mood than on the journey down. As soon as they came back within mobile reception range, her phone began picking up a series of texts sent over the preceding few days. Most of them were from Chris.

At first bantering and jolly, when no reply arrived, the messages passed into concerned and then, following her email of the previous day, to angry.

'Thought we had something special,' one read. 'Shame you didn't think so too.'

Another accused her of having led him on. 'I suppose you just wanted to spice up your love life at my expense,' read the bitter message.

Anna felt a brief stab of guilt as she quickly deleted all the messages. Then she began to feel resentful. True, she should have had the guts to tell him to his face that she wasn't about to dash off to Bristol to meet him in a hotel, but it wasn't as if she really owed him anything. After all, nothing had happened. Just a few emails and a couple of drunken snogs.

When other texts from him popped up in her inbox overnight, she deleted them without reading them. Sooner or later, she reasoned, he'd get the message.

The following day, Anna flew back to Portugal, desperate to be reunited with Dom. It seemed insane that just two weeks before she'd left him with barely a backward glance, impatient to be on her way to her ridiculous nostalgia-fest. Now she couldn't wait to see him again and for him to know how sorry she was and how much he meant to her. The journey seemed to go on forever.

Eventually, three hours after leaving London, Anna

was stumbling, light-headed through lack of sleep, into the arrivals hall. And there was Dom.

Never had she been more glad to see anybody in her whole life.

Dropping her bag, she ran over to him and flung her arms around him, not caring who saw the tears running down her face. She felt his familiar arms close tightly around her and she knew by the way his chest was heaving that he too was crying. 'That's it,' they promised each other in the car on the way home. 'No more secrets. A new beginning.'

Anna didn't even bother turning her phone on until much later that night. Once again, she had a stack of text messages waiting to be read. Once again, most were from Chris. Now, instead of being angry, they were deeply emotional, which Anna somehow found a lot more disturbing. He'd been so sure she was The One, he told her. Didn't she realise what she was throwing away? Anna grew increasingly uneasy as she scrolled through the heartfelt messages. 'We have so much history together,' read one. 'We were meant for each other.'

Dom read the messages over her shoulder with mounting anger. 'Are you sure there's not more to this than you've been telling me,' he snapped, glaring at her accusingly.

'I've told you the truth. All of it,' Anna pleaded. 'You have to believe me.' In desperation, she tried blocking

Chris' number from her phone and closed down the Hotmail email account. But still, he bombarded her with emails through her normal email address, which she couldn't change as she used it for work. Instead, she systematically deleted his messages without reading them and gradually they tailed off.

In the meantime, Anna and Dom were shakily rebuilding the relationship she'd almost destroyed with what she now described to Rosie as her 'stupid ego-stroke'. At first it was very hard. Although they were both full of good intentions to make this thing work, there were long-standing resentments to get over on both sides. Plus, every now and then Dom would lash out at her verbally about her 'boyfriend' back in England, vicious diatribes that seemed to come out of nowhere.

Gradually, and with a lot of effort on both sides, they began to heal the rifts between them. Dom really was trying to show her how much he cared – for the first time in years he was surprising her with little gifts or telling her how beautiful she looked. And Anna, in turn, was trying to prove to him that he could trust her again. When she was home her mobile phone was always out on the table in full view and Dom had access to all her Internet passwords.

Just as it looked as though things were settling down on to a more even keel, Chris Robinson came back into their lives.

It was 3.30am about four months after he'd first made contact with Anna when the home phone sounded. As always, Anna's immediate response was panic in case something had happened to one of their parents back home. Reaching groggily for the receiver, she managed a slightly slurred 'Hello' and then froze when she recognised the voice on the other end.

'Anna. It's me,' Chris said, urgently. 'Anna, you don't know what this is doing to me. I love you.'

Anna was horrified. 'How did you get this number?' she demanded, belatedly realising that with all the number-swapping that went on at the reunion, it wouldn't have been hard for him to find her. 'Listen, Chris, you've got to stop contacting me. I've told you, there's nothing at all between us. I love Dom.'

Chris wasn't discouraged. 'I know you're just saying that because *he's* there,' he told her. 'Don't worry. I understand.'

'I'm not,' Anna insisted. 'I'm saying it because it's true.'

Dom grabbed the phone. 'Look, you bastard. She doesn't want to talk to you. Leave her alone.'

He slammed down the receiver, but just a few seconds later, the phone rang again. As soon as Dom picked up the receiver, Chris started talking: 'I don't know what she's told you. But we're in love. I've known her twenty years longer than you, mate. You can't argue with fate.'

'Fuck off!' was Dom's predictable response.

Anna unplugged the phone. But that wasn't the last they'd heard of her childhood sweetheart. When phone calls and emails didn't yield any affect, Chris started calling mutual friends. 'He's clearly deranged,' Rosie marvelled, after receiving a series of calls from her love-sick former classmate. 'He says he's going to leave his wife for you.' Even Anna's parents became embroiled after Chris turned up drunk on their doorstep one night, trying to convince them that he and their daughter were made for one another.

'I'm so sorry I got us involved in all of this,' Anna would sob after yet another night's sleep was ruined by a long-distance call. Luckily, Dom could see for himself how distraught Anna was and Chris' campaign of stalking, obviously designed to drive them apart, actually had the opposite affect. After each intrusion on their lives, Anna and Dom felt closer together, bonded by a new-found desire to protect their relationship against any threats from the outside.

In fact, so united were they that one day, ten years after their first meeting, Dom asked her to marry him. 'Better late than never,' was Anna's choked response, as she threw her arms around his neck.

Anna was careful to add the news of her forthcoming wedding to her profile page on the Friends Reunited website, adding a comment about how thrilled she was that Dom was finally making an honest woman out of her.

To her considerable surprise, that seemed to do the trick. Apart from one very sarcastic 'congratulations on ruining my life' email she received via the website itself, Anna never heard anything more from Chris, at least not directly. Via various people she'd reconnected with at the reunion, she heard that he was still with his wife and, indeed, that she was expecting another baby, but there were no late-night phone calls, and she stopped bracing herself before logging onto her emails in the morning, for fear of what she'd find.

* * *

Anna and Dom returned to live in the UK and were married in 2007. Anna soon discovered she was pregnant with Ben, who is now a noisy one-year-old. 'Looking back on that whole episode with Chris Robinson, it just seems like it was someone else doing all those things,' she says now. 'That's the problem with these sorts of Internet sites. They allow you to step out of a real life you might be bored with, or worn down by, and become someone else. More than that, you become the person you used to be before life started to grind you down, only you make yourself more glamorous, more witty, more successful. That's the beauty of it – but that's also the danger.'

Since she's been back in the UK, Anna has been keeping a low profile when it comes to her old school.

'Obviously I'm still in touch with Rosie, and with one or two of the others from my old class,' she says. 'In fact, it's our thirty-year reunion next year – three decades since we left primary school.

'Somehow, though, I think I'll be giving that one a miss.'

CHAPTER ELEVEN
'YOU'VE GOT THE WRONG MAN'

tepping off the tiny plane at Alderney airport, Stephen Henshaw felt, as visitors always did, as if he'd entered into a different world. It wasn't just the startling pea-green countryside, rolling on towards the sea which, on this mild May morning, sparkled like a blue-sequinned blanket in every direction the eye could see. It was also the miniature size of everything, the way the buildings, the one town, even the airport itself looked to have been scaled down, as if shrunk in the wash. Despite its proud claim to be the third largest of the Channel Islands, Alderney still only managed to attain 5 km in one direction and 3 km in another, a compact nugget of land dropped randomly into the sea, just 11 km off the coast of Normandy.

Entering the one building that doubled both as

departures and arrivals hall, the impression continued of having, like Alice, crawled through a hidden door into a pocket-sized world from another time altogether. In place of a Starbucks or a Pret A Manger, there was a small buffet. The check-in section consisted of just two desks, and by the seats where the airport's few passengers waited patiently for their flights, there was a 'knit-while-you-wait' box, which invited them to while away the time knitting a square that would be eventually made into a quilt and donated to a third world country.

It was as if just the short flight from Guernsey, Alderney's larger, better-known neighbour, had transported the disembarking passenger across time zones to a place that the rest of the world had somehow left behind – a world where people still said hello when they passed you and you didn't need the famous sun dial outside to tell you that it was already, at midday, a glorious day.

But on this Friday, 2 May 2008, Stephen Henshaw wasn't in any mood to soak up the island's particular charms. He hadn't come to play golf on the island's immaculately well-kept nine-hole course on which players could swing a club in any direction and still keep their eyes trained on the horizon, or to patrol the coastline looking out for puffins, warblers, peregrines, or any of the other birdlife for which Alderney was famous. He'd come with only one aim. To find Jake Hamon.

❊   ❊   ❊

There were times when repairing boats could feel like a mug's game. On bleak winter afternoons, when the wind came blowing in off the sea, stinging your face like a slap, a man could be forgiven for thinking he'd be better off working in a shop or a bank or on the mainland, even. But on a sunny Friday lunchtime in early May, as the island geared up for extra bank holiday visitors, Jake Hamon was largely content.

A native Ridunian – the name given to those inhabitants who were born and bred on the island – Jake was all too familiar with the seasonal ups and downs of Alderney life. Like all the islanders, he'd learned to keep his mind occupied during the dreary winter months, playing with his band Skratch or just hanging out with his friends and kids. It was like they all spent six months of the year just biding time, treading water until the real fun started, round about this time of year when lengthening brighter days spelled weekends on the beach or long evenings in the garden.

This particular Friday, he was in buoyant mood. Not only because it was the start of summer, the time when the very air seems to hum in anticipation of summer, but also because he was nursing a secret. For weeks now, he'd been back in contact with a former girlfriend. They'd made contact through the social networking site Facebook and he still couldn't really believe they'd found each other again.

Tammy Henshaw (as she was now) had lived in

Alderney until she was 15, so she understood as well as anyone the way the island could get under your skin. They'd gone out together in their teens, but had lost touch when Tammy moved away. And now she was back in his life.

It had started with a tentative enquiry through the 'search' box on the site: 'Are you the same...?' Once they'd established that they were indeed the Jake and Tammy who'd known each other twenty years before, there followed a flurry of emails back and forth as they compared lives, hopes, dreams.

Tammy was married with two young children. The oldest, her eight-year-old son, was autistic, which could sometimes be difficult to deal with, and with her younger daughter being only three, life was pretty stressful. She lived in Grimsargh, near Preston, with her 39-year-old estate-agent husband Stephen.

Hearing about Jake's life on Alderney as a boat repairer, welder and part-time musician took her back to her time on the island, roaming the countryside and the beaches with the exhilarating freedom of youth. Jake's photo showed him to be largely unchanged, with long, sun-bleached hair and a twinkly smile, and she found herself thinking back to when she knew him before and life seemed so uncomplicated, and so accessible.

The Facebook messages soon turned into texts and then into phone conversations, as though they were trying to make up for all the long years of silence. It wasn't long before Tammy made a trip down to Alderney to revisit the forgotten faces of her youth – and to see Jake.

Whatever happened during that long overdue visit is, like the island itself, veiled in sea mist, its privacy protected by the timeless rocks and the endless tides. But one thing is clear. When Tammy flew back to Preston, she'd made a momentous decision – and one that was to turn her husband's world upside down, like an overturned bin whose contents never quite fit back inside again. She was going to move back to Alderney.

❊   ❊   ❊

At just 39, Stephen Hanshaw already felt like a broken man as he made his way out of Alderney airport. He'd recently lost his job, as far as he was concerned from having to take so much time out to look after the kids, and now he was in danger of losing his wife and probably his children too. All through the 300-mile trip from Manchester to Guernsey and then the short hop from Guernsey to Alderney, Stephen reflected on how badly things had gone wrong and how unfair it all was. He wasn't even being given a chance to try again. His life suddenly seemed like an untuned television, where nothing was in focus any more and nothing seemed to make sense. And, as far as he could see, there was one person to blame. Jake Hamon.

Finding out where he would be was the work of minutes in a place this small. Jake was a boat mechanic and welder, and it was pretty obvious whereabouts on Alderney a visitor was most likely to find him.

Approaching the harbour, Stephen didn't stop to admire the array of gleaming white yachts, dotted across the sea like rhinestones. Nor did he pause to observe the schooners with their sails fluttering slightly in the May breeze. His attention was focused on one point only.

Jake Hamon was kneeling down, his head bent over the boat he was working on, his long brown hair pushed back away from his face. So intently was he concentrating on what he was doing that he didn't notice the figure making its way determinedly towards him.

The first he knew of the presence of Stephen Henshaw, was when a fist caught him around the head, the sudden shock of pain sending him sprawling to the ground. For a fraction of a second, everything was black as he struggled to make sense of what had happened. Then, more out of instinct than anything else, he attempted to clamber to his feet, his head still reeling from the unheralded blow. But he'd barely managed to get upright before a brutal kick knocked him back down again. As he lay on the ground, a second kick landed in his back, causing a jolt of pain to shoot through him.

But overriding the physical agony was the psychological confusion. Who was this unknown assailant? Why was had he strolled up to him out of the blue on a perfectly ordinary day and launched into this bizarre, unprovoked attack? 'Stop, please stop,' Jake gasped, looking up at Stephen Henshaw through eyes clouded with pain and bewilderment. 'You've got the wrong man.'

If he'd been hoping for some response from this stranger – some gesture of apology or explanation, Jake was disappointed. 'Don't worry. I'm not going anywhere,' Stephen Henshaw told him, reeling off an address on the island. 'You can tell police where I'll be.'

Then he turned and walked away, just as abruptly as he'd arrived. Within seconds, it was as if he'd never been there – the sea still stretched out to the horizon as it had just a few minutes before, like a dark-blue tablecloth, studded with boats that glinted like shards of broken glass where they caught the sun.

But doubled up on the ground, Jake Hamon could be in no doubt that he'd just had a visitor. His head throbbed, there was an ominous ache in his abdomen and he didn't need a mirror to know that there was something seriously wrong with his jaw.

His head was still reeling, both from the pain and the shock. Who? Why? What? The questions whirled around his pounding head.

Later, while Jake was receiving eight painful stitches in his mouth and having his scalp wound cleaned up as much as possible, Stephen Henshaw was arrested at the address he'd left for the police. He'd made no attempt to leave the island, and offered no defence or resistance. It was as if his physical attack on Jake Hamon had drained him, not just of his anger, but also of some inner essence that had been keeping him going. Without it he was visibly diminished, as if something inside him had been siphoned off and chucked away.

※ ※ ※

In May 2008, a court in Alderney heard Stephen Henshaw plead guilty to unlawful and malicious wounding. Owing to his previous good character, he was given a three-month suspended sentence, thereby escaping jail – to the relief of both his wife, and his victim, neither of whom wanted to see this devoted, loving father go to prison. But while the legalities have now been settled, the emotional repercussions of the Alderney Facebook reunion continue to rumble on, as all concerned attempt to reassess their lives.

There's little doubt that rekindling a teenage romance from across the decades can be tempting. Who else shares that history? Who else knew you before jobs, responsibilities, mortgages shaped you into someone you no longer quite recognise? But sometimes when you attempt to plunge back into your past, you find your present trailing along behind you like an uninvited hitchhiker. You can go back to the place you once lived, you can go back to the people you once knew, but you can never really go back to the person you once were. Like it or not, you're now a product of the experiences you've had in the meantime, and the people you've since met. And when you try to burrow back in time, they'll all burrow right along with you – occasionally with catastrophic results.

CHAPTER TWELVE

THE LOVE THAT WAITED FIFTY YEARS

It couldn't have been a more perfect day. Just two weeks before, heavy storms had hit Penrith, Australia, and the River Nepean had flooded, completely submerging the boarding jetty. Marian had been anxiously scouring the long-range weather forecasts for clues as to whether more of the same lay in store, but she needn't have worried: 28 July 2007 dawned clear and sunny, the once-raging river now calm as a garden pond.

Boarding the cruiser, the *Penrith Platypus*, she was delighted to see so many dear, familiar faces. All her children and grandchildren were there, as were the friends she had made since arriving in Australia 26 years earlier, many of whom were expatriates from Northern Ireland, where she'd grown up. There too was

Michael's son John with his family, who were on holiday from England.

Moving closer to Michael, she squeezed his hand happily. 'Sometimes I still can't quite believe it,' she told him.

In truth, there were times it did all feel like a fairy tale – this magical wedding on board a beautiful boat cruising along in the Australian sunshine, the fact that she was a bride again at the age of 65 with a tiara nestling in her sun-bleached blonde hair. But in many ways the hardest thing of all to believe was that the man by her side, the man she was marrying in front of all these family and friends, was Michael Spathaky, who'd been her first boyfriend more than fifty years before.

❋   ❋   ❋

In the 1950s, Portadown College in Northern Ireland was in many ways a grammar school ahead of its time. Under the leadership of a forward-thinking head teacher, Donald Woodman, the pupils enjoyed a style of education that was creative and inclusive, forming strong bonds and friendships that in many cases would last them their entire lives.

Michael's father, Ron Spathaky, was a French teacher at the College. The family had moved from England when Michael was eight, so by the time he started at grammar school, he had no problem being accepted by the other 11-year-olds, many of whom he'd known from primary school

A group of them used to hang out together, riding their bikes at the weekends, making the occasional trip to the cinema. But as they got older, Michael began focusing his attention increasingly on one of his classmates in particular.

Marian Mitchell was intelligent and tall, with long, fair hair and a cheeky grin. She lived in Gilford, 5 miles from Portadown, travelling to school each day by bus. Like Michael, she was in the top stream at school and seemed to approach everything in life as a riotous adventure.

'Oh, here he comes again.'

Marian's friends nudged her as Michael Spathaky strolled awkwardly across the room, trying to adopt a studied air of nonchalance. He stopped self-consciously in front of her.

'Would you like to...?'

Ever since they'd entered the third year and were old enough to attend the ballroom dance classes held in the school hall, Michael had been regularly making that agonising trip across the no man's land that divided the girls on one side and the boys on the other. Of course, he hadn't only invited Marian to dance – that would have been far too embarrassing. Other girls had been singled out for a dutiful shuffle around the assembly hall, but Marian was far and away his favourite partner.

For Marian's part, she was always relieved when she spotted Michael weaving across the hall in her direction. As is so often the case with 13- and 14-year-olds, she and her friends towered above most of the boys in her year, and it was always a pleasure to dance with someone whose head didn't stop at her armpit.

'He really likes you,' her friends giggled.

So when Marian opened her locker one day to find a note from Michael inside asking her to meet him, she wasn't totally surprised. Years later, they would argue over when this was. Michael maintains he first slipped a note into her locker in October 1955, while Marian says it all started with a Valentine's card the following February. But whatever the timing, it did the trick.

Michael began cycling the 5 miles to Gilford every Friday night. Marian, whose mother believed 13 was far too young to be stepping out with a boy, would make excuses to go out and meet him, pretending to be visiting her friend Norma. Being a good, well-brought-up girl, Marian wouldn't have considered lying outright to her parents, so she would indeed pay a visit to the very indulgent Norma, before scooting off to meet up with Michael afterwards.

Later, they would sometimes meet on a Saturday, when there was far less need for excuses. This was the era where children routinely set off from home on their bikes in the watery light of an early morning and weren't expected home until the sun went down. Untroubled by having to think of covering stories, Michael and Marian would stroll to the banks of the River Bann and spend the day skimming stones and holding hands.

Being 1956, nothing untoward happened between the two classmates. The two would hold hands while they were out, or in the darkness of the weekly film club at school, but they never progressed to the kissing stage. Not that Michael wasn't tempted, but every time he worked up his courage to lean in towards her, at the last minute his nerve would fail. Marian was such a tomboy, she gave the impression she wouldn't go in for all that soppy stuff.

Then came the bombshell.

'Dad's been offered another job back in England,' Michael told Marian dramatically. 'We're moving to Norwich.'

It was a blow in as much as the two were close friends who would miss one another's company, but the truth was that, being 14, the news of the premature ending of their romance didn't exactly send either spiralling into a trough of depression.

While Michael was sad to be leaving the friends he'd made over the last six years, he couldn't help feeling a little excited to be going back to England, which seemed to him to be rich in new possibilities. Marian, for her part, would be surrounded by the friends she'd known since early childhood, and certainly wouldn't have a chance to feel lonely. So the parting, when it came, was hardly the stuff of *Casablanca* or *Brief Encounter*.

'I'll write to you, all the time,' promised Michael. True to his word, his letters started arriving regularly at Marian's Gilford home. Her mother, who believed it slightly inappropriate for a girl of Marian's age to be receiving letters from a boy, insisted on vetting them. In the event, it was Marian's mum, rather than the slightly disapproving Marian herself, who was won over by Michael's flowery endearments.

'My darling Marian,' he'd begin. Marian's mother would visibly melt as she read on, while Marian herself would usually make some dismissive comment about it being so 'soppy'.

Michael threw himself wholeheartedly into his new life at Norwich School. Portadown College had given him a good start academically and his rugby skills were noticed early. He made a few changes to his persona, wearing his glasses full time and changing his name from Michael to Mike. But there were some disappointments. For a start, he was at an all-boys school, with a much more conventional, conservative ethos than the progressive Portadown College. He found himself homesick for the untroubled, fun-filled school life he'd known in Ireland and for the friends he'd left behind. Particularly Marian.

The trouble was that Michael's family, like many at the time, didn't have a phone, and neither did Marian's. He could have arranged to call her at a phone box, but that would have taken a week's pocket money just on one call. So, unable to talk to her in person, he continued writing doggedly, telling her about what he'd done at school, asking about people they both knew.

But, as everyone knows, a year is a lifetime when you're 15 or 16. Michael still thought of Marian as his girlfriend, but there seemed to be less and less to talk to her about. He had a whole new life that didn't involve her, and it was difficult to keep asking about people whose faces he was already beginning to forget.

Finally, two years after he moved back to England, Michael stopped writing altogether. He realised it was futile to keep hankering back to what had been, after all, just a passing childhood friendship. He was 16 now, and wanted a real flesh-and-blood girlfriend, not a scrawled signature on the bottom of a letter.

He felt bad about it, of course, but as a child of the decidedly un-touchy-feely 1950s, he just didn't have the language to tell Marian in an emotionally honest way about how he was feeling. Easier just to put off writing altogether until so much time had gone past that it would have seemed awkward to have resumed again.

Back in Portadown, Marian became vaguely aware that she hadn't received a letter from Michael for a while. In the back of her mind, she kept expecting to hear something, but when it became obvious the postman wasn't going to be delivering any more envelopes with that familiar handwriting, she was philosophical about it. She and her family had moved from Gilford to Portadown not long before and she suspected maybe Michael had lost her new address. In some ways it was a bit of a relief. It had become harder and harder to think of things to say recently, and the letters, which had started out so exuberantly, had become rather stilted affairs.

It was June 1958 when Michael stopped writing. Later, Marian would joke he'd timed it deliberately so he wouldn't have to buy her a birthday present in July.

The following year, Marian left school and immediately took a job working as a Civil Service clerk based in Stormont. Each morning, she'd get up early to travel the hour-and-a-half into Belfast, not returning until well after dark. She didn't have time to wonder what had happened to the boy she'd waved goodbye to as schoolgirl and whose letters had so abruptly dried up.

At the age of 17 1/2, she met local man Sammie Chambers, then an apprentice lathe turner, at a dance in Portadown. The two fell in love and, as was common practice in the early 1960s, lost little time in getting married, tying the knot in 1962.

In those days, married women were not allowed to

work in the Civil Service in Northern Ireland. Jobs were scarce, and it was felt they were taking work from men and unmarried women who needed it, instead of being supported by their husbands. So Sammie and Marian ended up moving to England, where the regulations governing Civil Service jobs weren't quite so draconian. Marian's elder sister already lived there in south London, so they had plenty of support. When Marian turned up at the Tooting labour exchange to register for work, she was amazed to be offered a job there on the spot.

Life was good for the hard-working Irish couple, and the birth of their three children cemented what was a very contented marriage. But in the early 1980s, they decided they'd like a break. They'd both worked solidly since leaving school and hadn't had the chances to travel and broaden their horizons that many younger people now take for granted. They decided to move to Australia for a couple of years. The children – Dawn, 12, Gilly, 10, and Garry, 8 – were still young enough to be uprooted from school without too drastic an effect on their education, and Marian and Sammie were confident they could find work.

The family set off for their big adventure in 1981 and all seemed to be going to plan when both found work easily, and the children slotted into schools with few dramas. But, as the two years came to a close, they discovered going back to England might not be quite as straightforward as they'd assumed. Due to differences in the education system, the children were now six months behind their UK peers. Also, the Australian dollar had gone down against the pound, meaning they'd take a financial loss if they returned home. By this time Sammie had a job he enjoyed, so after much debate and soul-searching, the Chambers family decided to stay.

Thousands of miles away, Michael's life had followed a remarkably similar pattern to that of his erstwhile childhood sweetheart. After his correspondence with Marian had petered out, he'd met his future wife, Diana, in January 1960. Coincidentally, it was ballroom dancing classes again that brought the two together.

The relationship flourished even when Michael went away to Manchester University to study physics, and the couple were married in August 1964. On their wedding day itself, they travelled to Leicester, where Michael was due to take a year's teacher training course. Much in the same way that Marian and Sammie had approached their Australia venture, the idea was never to stay indefinitely. Michael would do his training, then they'd return to Norwich to start their lives properly. But, as with all best-laid plans, this one soon began to unravel. Diana, who'd got a job as a secretary straight away on arriving in Leicester, decided to follow Michael into teacher training. The couple made friends, laid down roots. Before they knew it, they had two children in local schools and their lives were interwoven into the local community.

And so they stayed in Leicestershire. Michael moved into community education, climbing the ranks until he became a college vice-principal, and Diana carved herself out a career as a well-respected special needs teacher.

❊ ❊ ❊

The years passed and, on different sides of the world, Marian and Michael continued living their strangely parallel lives, bringing up their families and participating in the life of the communities around them. Every now and then they'd think back to Portadown days, mostly when there was something on the telly that reminded them of Ireland or of their schooldays. Marian in particular was prone to reminiscing because Sammie and she, having grown up in the same area, shared so many of the same memories. On the whole though, the past was a luxury they were usually too busy to indulge in.

It was in 1997 that the first heavy clouds appeared over the horizon of Marian and Sammie's Australian idyll. Always a keen sportsman, Sammie had been out playing tennis with a friend. 'I was a bit uncoordinated out there today,' he said to Marian, rubbing his right foot gingerly. 'It felt like I had a club foot or something.'

Over the next few days, the problem got worse, to the point where Sammie was manually moving his foot from the accelerator to the brake when he drove the car.

'Go to the doctor,' Marian urged him.

But Sammie was convinced it was nothing serious. 'I'll make an appointment with the chiropractor,' he told her.

The chiropractor was worried, echoing Marian's concerns. 'You've got to go and see a doctor about that.'

Sammie was still sure there was nothing seriously wrong with him, but in August 1997, a scan revealed the unthinkable. The fighting-fit 57-year-old was suffering from a brain tumour.

It was a crushing diagnosis, but Sammie was one of nature's positive thinkers. He was sure that the surgery he was booked in for on 24 August would sort him out. The operation took place on the eve of Sammie's 58th birthday and from the minute he came round from the anaesthetic, he was characteristically convinced it had been a success. His optimism was infectious and Marian found herself also unable to countenance any outcome other than Sammie coming out of hospital and resuming life just as he had left off.

For a while, it seemed their buoyancy was well founded. Sammie seemed to recover well and, even though they were told three weeks after the operation that surgeons hadn't been able to remove all of the tumour and that it was so aggressive he had only a four per cent chance of recovery, they fervently believed he would be one of that lucky four per cent.

'We're going to beat this thing,' Sammie would say, and hearing the conviction in his voice, Marian couldn't help but believe it too. But in December, Sammie began having problems getting up in the mornings. For an energetic, vigorous man, this lassitude was almost unheard of. Still Marian kept any reservations at bay, making sure he took the increased dosage of anti-inflammatories the doctors prescribed, which brought him periods of good health, although these seemed to be getting shorter and shorter.

In February 1998, Sammie's two sisters flew from Ireland to Australia to visit, and seeing them gave him a much-needed boost. Marian had given up work as soon as Sammie received his diagnosis, and together the couple made trips to different parts of Australia, making the most of their time together. 'We're on top of this,' Marian would tell well-wishers, confidently.

But on 21 June 1998, Sammie died. Despite the bleak prognosis, the brain surgery and the four per cent chance of recovery he'd been given, Marian was still shell-shocked. No matter how much you think you've prepared for something, no one is ever really ready for the reality of bereavement, particularly not after 36 years of marriage.

But she still had her youngest child, Garry, who was a

TAMMY COHEN

tennis coach, living at home. He provided company, invaluable emotional support and also a structure to her day. There were still meals to be cooked, bills to be paid. Marian had always lived by the philosophy that you kept your emotions private, rather than upsetting those around you. She grieved into herself, but outwardly she carried on going through the motions of everyday life, and gradually re-accustomed herself to this new reality, no matter how unwanted.

Volunteering for charity work helped her focus her mind on other people over the following months and years, and she threw herself into working for organisations such as Meals on Wheels and the National Trust. Family and friends rallied round her, with her elder sister making the long trip over from England. Marian herself travelled abroad, visiting friends in Canada and making plans to visit England.

Yet no matter how full her life, there were inevitably times when she found herself on her own, with time to kill that she didn't want to spend dwelling on painful memories or watching mindless TV. Instead, she began surfing the Internet, amazed at the world of possibilities that opened up to her with the click of a computer mouse.

When a friend told her about a new website that had started up in the UK, putting old school friends in touch with one another, she couldn't resist a look. Keying in the name of her old primary school, she shrieked with delight when a list of names came up, many of whom she recognised immediately. It didn't seem real that she could sit in her home in Sydney and reconnect with people from whom she was separated by thousands of miles and half a century!

So entranced was Marian by the new world opened up by Friends Reunited that when she was back in England in October 2001, visiting an old friend, she insisted it would be a laugh for the two of them to go onto the website together. Typing in Portadown College this time, she perused the list of names and then stopped short.

'I don't believe it!' she shrieked. '*Michael Spathaky*!'

Sometimes, going through the class lists, she had come to a name and hesitated slightly, wondering if that was the same Andrew or Christine she'd known as a child, but with an unusual name like Spathaky, there were no such doubts.

'Send him a message,' her friend urged.

Marian didn't need persuading. She hadn't thought about Michael in a long time, but seeing his name had brought back to her in a welcome rush the memories of that faraway, innocent time where they'd all been young and carefree, and all that was needed for a great day out was a few sandwiches and a bicycle.

'Do you remember me?' she wrote, realising too late that the message would be sent from her friend's email address, which might prove confusing. But she needn't have worried.

Michael and Diana had retired early from the education service and were now running a small Internet business from their home in Oadby. On most days, Diana was also looking after their grandchildren. Michael was at his computer when the email came in. Immediately, he printed it out and rushed downstairs to show Diana.

'What are you waiting for?' she chided. 'Get her over for lunch.'

Michael returned to his keyboard. 'Of course I remember you!' he typed enthusiastically. 'I can't believe it! Is it really you, Marian? Oh my God! Memories, memories… Happy memories of '56.'

A quick flurry of emails followed, in which each caught up a little on the outline of the other's life. Michael and Diana insisted that Marian should come to visit them in Oadby before she went back to Australia. 'Come for lunch,' he entreated.

So it was that, a few days later, Marian found herself on a train pulling into Leicester station. Knowing that when it came to picking her out from the crowd he'd be relying solely on memory, she mischievously she took off the distinctive yellow jacket she'd told him to look out for and put it in her bag, wondering if he'd recognise her without it.

The last passenger off the train, Marian caught sight

of a middle-aged man standing outside the ticket barrier, peering anxiously past the disembarking throng. She'd have known him anywhere. He looked the spitting image of his dad!

Michael also recognised her immediately. Funny, he'd been worrying he wouldn't. After all, he hadn't seen her in 45 years and, without any photograph to remind him, he'd only retained the haziest recollection of her – a cloud of fair hair, a big smile. But as soon as he saw her face, all the memories came flooding back and any apprehensions he'd had melted away.

Right from the start, the conversation flowed easily, without any awkwardness despite the huge time lapse since they'd last seen each other. Diana and Marian took to each other immediately and the three passed a pleasant day, chatting over lunch with Diana and Mike's grandchildren, then taking a walk in the nearby countryside, reminiscing.

'What was Mike like in those days?' Diana wanted to know.

Marian tried to remember, but it was all a bit vague – and besides, it wasn't as if she and Michael had been seriously dating. 'We were just children,' she explained. 'We never even kissed.'

'Maybe we should do it now,' Michael joked, as they were taking photographs, earning himself a playful reprimand from Diana.

'It's incredible how strong the bonds are from those formative years,' Michael remarked to Diana when Marian had left.

Marian had invited them both out to stay with her in Sydney and the Spathakys discussed the possibility seriously. Having been out to Australia on holiday a few years before, they'd been struck by just how much there was to see – the sheer scope and scale of the landscape had awed them. Plus, Marian had a large home with a separate guest living space upstairs.

'Maybe we should think about taking her up on it,' Diana mused.

Sadly, it was not to be.

Marian kept in touch with Michael by email and over the months following her visit, she noticed a recurring note of worry creeping in to what had until then been quite jovial light-hearted banter. Diana had been acting slightly oddly, Michael revealed. She'd forgotten things – dates of grandchildren's birthday parties, road directions. She'd come back from the supermarket confused and empty-handed, having forgotten what she'd gone there for, and had started complaining of pains in her legs, particularly walking downhill. On a mini-break in April 2002, when Michael had been laid up with flu, she hadn't wanted to leave the hotel without him, which was most unlike her, and had taken a wrong turning on the motorway while driving home.

On the other side of the world, Marian read Michael's concerns with a growing feeling of disquiet. She'd read about the symptoms of early Alzheimer's. She worried it could be that.

In the end, when the diagnosis came in May 2002, it was the worst possible. Diana, like Sammie, had a brain tumour. After her operation, she too had been given only a year to live, cruelly hearing the stark prognosis while she was on her own in a hospital some distance away.

Marian's heart contracted when she heard the news. She knew only too well what the following months held in store for Michael, and she wished she there were something she could say or do to help him. But ultimately she knew this was something he was going to have to find his own way through, heartbreaking though it would be.

For the next few months, Marian tried to offer whatever support she could. Michael would email or phone her once a week to give her an update on what was happening, or to ask her for advice or just to have someone listen to him. Of course, he had his children close by, who were a huge support, but sometimes being able to talk to someone who was outside the situation really helped, particularly when they'd been through precisely the same thing themselves and knew, without being told, all about the frustration and the loneliness and the sheer despair you go through when your life partner is fading away in front of your eyes.

Desperately ill, Diana went into a hospice but left a couple of weeks later after begging Michael to take her home.

In October 2002, came the phone call Marian had been dreading. Michael was in floods of tears as he told her Diana had passed away, five-and-a-half months after being handed that initial brutal diagnosis.

What can you say to somebody who's just seen the foundations of his life swept from under him? Marian felt inadequate as she tried to describe to him how she herself had coped when she'd been in the same position, and how it seemed like a cliché but, in the end, life did go on.

The following weeks and months were a nightmare for Michael. While Marian had had her son still living at home and a structure to her days, Michael seemed to have lost his internal compass without Diana. For the past five months his whole life had been built around caring for her, and now he was faced with an emptiness no amount of well-wishing friends and relatives could fill.

His children were a big help, but they had their own lives to lead with young families to look after and partners they could lean on for support. Increasingly, Michael found himself turning to Marian, drawing comfort from being able to talk to someone for whom he didn't have to wear a brave face, someone who knew without having to be told exactly what he was going through.

For Michael, that Christmas passed in a blur of grief, but as 2002 slipped soundlessly into 2003, he knew he had to start thinking differently. Diana was gone and she wasn't coming back: the life he'd known before was gone forever. It was up to him to build a new life now.

He began to entertain thoughts of having a complete change of scenery. The last few months had been so harrowing, he knew it would do him good to get away for a while from the place that was now so imbued with memories. There was only one obvious destination.

'Of *course*,' Marian exclaimed when Michael asked shyly if the invitation she'd extended to him and Diana still stood. She knew he'd not been coping too well since Diana's death, and was sure a bit of distance couldn't help but do him good. Besides, his visit would coincide with the Rugby World Cup, which was being held in Sydney in October/November. What better distraction from the punishing relentlessness of bereavement?

Michael arrived in Australia in October 2003 and, right from the start, he and Marian fell into the easy friendship of people who've known one another a long time. Together they explored the region, with Marian taking her visitor to places most tourists never see. In the evenings they'd have dinner out in the garden or sit side by side watching television in comfortable silence.

For two outgoing people who'd been prematurely robbed of their life companions, it was a comfort they hadn't really been expecting, and the bond between the two former childhood sweethearts strengthened over the weeks and ultimately months Michael spent at Marian's home.

For Michael who, from the start, had thought of Australia as the turning of a new page after the traumas of the preceding year, the deepening relationship was a source of great joy and an affirmation that after all, life could still be good again.

Marian was more circumspect, knowing what Michael had just been through and how emotionally wrung out he must be feeling.

In February 2004, a few days before Michael was due to fly back to England, he took Marian out for dinner at the Sydney Tower, a revolving restaurant with a panoramic view at the top of the highest building in Sydney. Michael ordered an expensive champagne, but he was strangely tense during the meal. Then, during the dessert course, he turned to her with an unreadable expression on his face. He was certainly acting very strangely, but still she wasn't prepared for the question that fell from his lips:

'Marian, will you marry me?'

Marriage! She was absolutely reeling. Sure, they got on very well, and their shared childhood memories brought an extra depth to their friendship, but to her mind there was no way Michael was in the right frame of mind to be deciding how he felt about anything, let alone how he was going to spend the rest of his life.

'How long have I got to answer?' she replied.

'It would be good if I knew by Friday,' he said. That was the day he was due to fly home to England.

On the Friday, Marian drove him to the airport with a feeling of regret mixed with healthy resignation. She knew he'd return when he could and, like him, she had her own life to lead.

Making their way through the airport concourse, Marian found herself perplexed when Michael suddenly stopped outside an expensive jewellery shop.

'Come on,' she chided him. 'What's keeping you?'

They moved on to an airport pizzeria, where Michael turned to her and said: 'If you say "Yes" now, you can choose an engagement ring at that jewellers and I'll buy it now. Then we'll know it's for ever.'

He thought she hesitated. Long enough for him to think that if she said 'No' this time, there was still a chance in the future. Eventually she said, 'It's too soon. You can't possibly know what you want right now.'

Michael tried to tell her that he knew exactly what he wanted, but Marian was adamant. She was still shell-shocked by the time she got back home and started trying to make sense of what had happened. Of course it was flattering, and of course it was tempting. But what would Michael's family think? After all, it was little more than a year since Diana's death. And how on earth could he tell what he really wanted when his emotions were still all over the place? When you're as needy as Michael had been, there's a risk that you'll run to any port in the storm. And Marian certainly didn't want that to be her. Then there were the logistics of the whole thing – living on two different continents wasn't ideal for a couple planning to get wed. The more she thought about it, the more problems there seemed to be. No, far better to remain as they were.

Michael was disappointed by Marian's refusal, but not too downhearted. Marian Chambers, née Mitchell, would find he could be very persistent when he put his mind to something.

In fact over the next few years, Michael and Marian spent more and more time together. They had agreed to meet again soon and it was not long before Marian was planning a visit to the UK. She booked a flight for May 2004 with a stopover in Paris and suggested that Michael fly over to meet her there.

They stayed in a cosy little hotel near the Eiffel Tower. They went to the Musée d'Orsay and the Musée Rodin, took a trip on the Seine and wandered hand in hand through the Jardin des Tuileries. They had romantic tête-à-têtes in little restaurants on the Left Bank. It didn't really matter where they went – they were in Paris, in the spring.

They had separate planes to catch to England and

Marian spent a few days with her sister in Essex before travelling to Michael's home in Oadby. She spent time getting to know Michael's family, who all lived nearby. But after less than a month in England, Marian had to go home because her eldest daughter, Dawn, had been taken ill.

Michael made the long, tedious journey to Sydney several times. Before the year was out, he had had another three-month stay with Marian in Sydney, returning to England to celebrate his dad's 90th birthday in November. Then, in 2005, he arranged a house swap with a young Sydney family so that he spent practically the whole year Down Under. Marian and he split the time between her house and his exchange house, which because of its pool was a favourite in hot weather and ideal for family gatherings. In July, Michael's daughter Jane came over from England with her husband Chris and their two children for a four-week stay.

There were still the headaches over visas. Michael had to travel to New Zealand and back halfway through the year to satisfy Australian visa requirements. It was quite an inconvenience, but still, every time he broached the subject of marriage, which would have sorted out the vexing visa question, Marian demurred. Where would they live? She had her family in Australia, he had his in the UK – how could they possibly be together without upsetting one set of children?

While Michael was planning another trip to Sydney in 2006, Marian suggested that she would travel back with him when he returned to the UK, as she had been invited to the wedding of a friend's daughter in Eastbourne. He bought a single ticket to Sydney so that they could get return tickets together for the trip to England. Michael felt this marked a new stage in their relationship, as it meant they would be together continuously both for his visit to Australia and hers to Europe.

They agreed on a stopover in Copenhagen this time, another romantic venue, before flying into Birmingham where Marian's younger sister met them and drove them to Michael's house in Oadby. Michael was determined to give Marian a great time in the UK, which started with a 'magical mystery tour' of the beautiful county of Rutland. Other trips followed: to the Derbyshire Peaks; the Lake District; around the south of England from Kent to Devon visiting various friends; the wedding in Eastbourne; and then a three-week trip to Ireland to see Michael's brother Dave in the south-west and all Marian's friends and relations in the north. There were also numerous gatherings of both their families.

After a hectic three months they returned to Australia, where Michael spent another six months until March 2007. They had now been together for nearly three years except for two periods of three and two months respectively. Michael had started to put down some roots in Australia. He had bought a car and a small sailing boat, which he raced on Sydney's Upper Harbour. Marian and he were regarded as a couple by their friends and families in both countries. But Michael had stopped asking Marian about marriage. The rejections hurt too much. 'If you change your mind,' he had said, 'It'll have to be you who proposes.'

Michael returned to England alone for a three-month visit to see his family. His return flight to Australia was booked for June 2007. Meanwhile, Marian and he had already invited Michael's son, John, his wife Alison and their two children for a holiday in July.

It was this planned visit that finally changed Marian's mind about marriage. Marian was talking to her younger daughter, Gilly, in Canberra about John's forthcoming visit. 'If we *were* to get married, I suppose it would be really good to do it at a time when Michael's family could be here,' Marian mused.

Gilly looked at her sternly. 'Mum, if you think like that, why on earth don't you just bite the bullet?'

Marian blinked at her in surprise, trying to think of a reason to say 'no', but to her great surprise she couldn't find one.

Early in the morning on 16 April 2007, the phone rang in Michael's home in Oadby. 'I was thinking,' Marian began. 'If we *were* to get married, how would you like to do it when John and Alison come out in July so that you have some family support?'

Still half asleep, Michael couldn't quite get his thoughts to process what he'd just heard. As Marian waited anxiously, the unexpected silence seemed to echo down the phone line. Then Michael cleared his throat. 'Are you asking what I think you're asking?'

'Erm, I think so...'

There was another silence, and then: 'Yes, yes, YES!'

More than fifty years after he'd slipped that note into 13-year-old Marian Mitchell's locker, it seemed Michael Spathaky was finally making some progress.

❋   ❋   ❋

All the guests agreed they'd never been to such a magical wedding. The weather – often unpredictable in Australia in July, the beginning of winter – smiled down on the double-decked *Penrith Platypus* as it glided along the River Nepean. On either side, the wild, natural landscape of the Nepean Gorge in the Blue Mountain National Park rose up, towering over them in a mass of sandstone, rock and eucalyptus trees whose oil produces the blue haze after which the area was named.

On board, the 55 guests, including four of the couple's five children and seven of their nine grandchildren, listened as the celebrant conducted a civil wedding service against the stunning backdrop.

The menus and invitations were adorned with a finely sketched drawing of two pink-breasted birds, galahs, which Marian and Michael had chosen for their motif because of their predilection for sitting in pairs on the electricity wires outside Marian's Sydney home, and cooing lovingly to one another.

Among the tight throng of family and friends was one unexpected guest. Rebecca Foley had also grown up in Portadown and made the big move to Australia. Although she and Marian had never crossed paths, Rebecca had known Sammie and his sisters as children in Portadown. When she'd read about the wedding in the local Portadown paper, which her family sent her faithfully each week, she'd decided she had to go down to the jetty to wish Marian and Michael luck, even though she'd never even met them. 'Well, now you're here, you must come too,' Marian insisted, unaware then that Rebecca would soon become a firm friend.

As the happy couple had diplomatically decided to divide their time equally between their homes in Australia and the UK, it made sense to hold another part of the wedding celebration in England. No sooner had the photos from the July wedding been positioned in albums in Marian's Sydney living room and the thank-you letters sent out than they were on a plane again, heading to Michael's home town of Oadby. There, on

Saturday, 6 October, at St Peter's Church in Oadby, there was a blessing service conducted by an old friend of Marian's, followed by a reception at Beauchamp College, where Mike had worked for 25 years, nicely rounded off by a ceilidh.

And because good things always come in threes, they also managed to squeeze in a third celebration in between those two events – a party organised for them back in Northern Ireland by Sammie's two sisters in a wonderful gesture of generosity.

* * *

Now settled into their enviable two-country lifestyle, Mr and Mrs Michael Spathaky can't believe just how far they've come in order to, in effect, complete what they started more than half a century ago.

'I'd always regarded those years in Ireland as the golden era of my childhood,' says Michael now. 'The fact that Marian was my girlfriend and we share the same memories of teachers and classmates gives us a very special bond.'

Marian, for her part, can't get over how, after parting as children, she and Michael led such parallel but completely separate lives until a website brought them back together again.

'Because we shared those early years, there's not a whole lot we don't know about each other and that gives our relationship a depth it mightn't have had if we'd only known each other a few years. Isn't it wonderful the way life turns full circle?'